View here the Shadow whose Ingenious Hand
Hath dranne exact the Province Mary Land
Display'd her Glory in such Sccenes of Witt
That those that read must fall in Love with it
For which his Labour hee deserves the praise
As well as Poets, doe the wreath of Bays.

Anno Do: 1666. Ætatis Suæ 28.   H.W.

GEORGE ALSOP, from the Portrait *in the* Original Edition of 1666.

The portrait of Alsop above is from the Mereness edition of *A Character of the Province of Mary-Land*. The reproduction of the portrait in Mereness' book is sharper than that of Shea's edition, and is here included for the convenience of the reader.

A
CHARACTER
OF THE
PROVINCE
OF
MARY-LAND

1666

BY

GEORGE ALSOP

FACSIMILE REPRODUCTION
WITH AN INTRODUCTION

BY

ROBERT A. BAIN, Ph. D.

University of North Carolina
at
Chapel Hill

Bainbridge, New York

YORK MAIL–PRINT, INC.

1972

YORK MAIL-PRINT, INC.

CORNER PRUYN & PARSONS STS.

BAINBRIDGE, NEW YORK

JOHN R. COMPTON, GENERAL EDITOR

ISBN 0-913126-03-9

Manufactured In The U.S.A.

CONTENTS

060480

The World's in a heap of troubles and confusion, and while
they are in the midst of their changes and amazes, the best
way to give them the bag, is to go out of the World and
leave them. I am now bound for *Mary-Land,* and I am told
that's a New World, but if it prove no better than this, I
shall not get much by my change; but before I'le revoke
my Resolution, I am resolv'd to put it to adventure, for I
think it can hardly be worse then this is.[1]

So wrote George Alsop, then twenty years old, to his father from
aboard a ship at Gravesend on Sept. 7, 1658. From all appear-
ances, Alsop found Maryland a better world, for upon his return
to England after more than four years in the colony, he published
A Character of the Province of Mary-Land (London, 1666), a
little book celebrating Lord Baltimore's settlement as *"The
Miracle of this Age."*

What little we know about Alsop's life comes from his book.
The facts are few; the inferences drawn from these facts have
been more numerous.

The facts seem to be these. Of humble parentage, Alsop was
born in 1638, probably in London, and was the elder of two sons
in his family. About the age of eighteen, he began a "Handicraft
Apprenticeship" of some sort in London. Unlike many apprentices
of his day, Alsop learned to read and write, and even knew some
Latin. For reasons not entirely clear, he sailed for Maryland in
1658. Alsop's Royalist sympathies probably prompted his migration, but there may have been other reasons for his leaving England. Arriving in Maryland in January of 1659, he became an
indentured servant to Thomas Stockett, a humane master who
settled in Baltimore County. Alsop's indenture was for four years,
but nowhere in his book does he state the precise nature of his
service. It has been suggested that Stockett employed him in the
Indian trade. Near the end of his fourth year in Maryland, Alsop
became ill and nearly died. By April of 1663, he had recovered
and sometime thereafter returned to England. In 1666, at the age
of twenty-eight, he published *A Character of the Province of*

Mary-Land and then disappeared from view.[2]

The book Alsop wrote about his Maryland adventures contains two dedicatory epistles, a Preface to the Reader, four numbered chapters, and two additional sections. The first chapter, *"The Scituation, and plenty of the Province,"* describes briefly the landscape and animal life of Maryland and lauds the colony for its "super-abounding plenty"; the second chapter, *"The Laws, Customs, and natural Demeanor of the Inhabitant,"* depicts the Marylanders as tolerant, loyal subjects, who work hard and appreciate plain good sense. The third chapter, *"The worst and best Usage of a Mary-Land Servant, opened in view,"* defends the indenture system and puffs the opportunities for the poor and the unemployed tradesmen of England in America. Chapter Four, *"The Traffique, and Vendable Commodities of the Countrey,"* opens with a digression in praise of trade and then discusses the tobacco trade and other commerce of the plantation. The next section, viewed by one editor as Alsop's most valuable contribution, is "A Relation of the Customs, Manners, Absurdities, and Religion of the *Susquehanock Indians* in and near *Mary-Land*." Here Alsop records his "occular experimental view" of Susquehannock culture, describing what he observed "while I was amongst these naked *Indians*." The last section comprises twelve letters that Alsop wrote to family and friends in England. These letters are dated by the day of writing, not by the year. Though the genuineness of these letters has been questioned, no convincing argument has been made against their authenticity. Also in Alsop's book are two hundred and thirty-eight lines of original verse, and another seventy-two lines of complimentary verse, apparently contibuted by three unidentified friends.

Alsop's book is important for a number of reasons. First, it is one of the three contemporary published accounts of a "half dozen or so pieces of promotional writing during Maryland's first quarter century."[3] The other two published promotional tracts, quite different in manner and style, are Father Andrew White's *A Relation of Maryland* (London, 1635) and John Hammond's *Leah and Rachel; or, The Two Fruitfull Sisters Virginia, and Maryland* (London, 1656). Second, Howard Mumford Jones notes that in the promotional literature "one would search in vain to find out what the indentured servant thought and felt,"[4] but Alsop served a four-year indentureship and his book is "the only Southern promotional narrative written by an indentured servant."[5] *A Character* may not tell precisely what the indentured servant thought and felt since its aim seems to have been promotion of migration to the colony, but Alsop viewed his servitude as an easy yoke, one "not to me so slavish, as a two years Servitude of a Handicraft Apprenticeship was here in *London*" (p. 54). Third, though Alsop calls his book a history, it is a promotional tract, but some parts of the book—especially the letters, the chapter on servitude, and the discourse on the Indians—possess characteristics of the personal narrative, albeit a highly un-Puritan or un-Quaker narrative. Alsop's insistence that he writes from "an experimental knowledge of the Country, and not from any imaginary supposition" and his use of the first person pronoun, particularly in the chapter on servitude, give these sections of his narrative a highly personal tone not usually associated with promotional writing.[6] Fourth, Alsop's style is unlike that of nearly all colonial writing, for he rejects the plain style of the day for the more ornate, the more playful, and the more bombastic. Commentators on the book have disagreed about the effectiveness of Alsop's style, but many compare Alsop's prose to that of Nathaniel Ward's *The Simple Cobbler of Agawam* (London, 1647). Finally, *A Character of the Province of Mary-Land* is one of the early bawdy books written about America. Some commentators have charged Alsop with obscenity. His scatological outbursts at times sound harsh to the delicate ear, and his allusions to London lowlife, wombs, and sex are numerous. Hugh T. Lefler has wryly observed that Alsop's book "had the three ingredients that might have made it a best seller three centuries later—sin, sex, and the South."[7] Perhaps the best comparison would be with Thomas Morton's *The New English Canaan* (Amsterdam, 1637), a book which includes some bawdy verse and unflatteringly off-color comments about the Separatists of Plymouth Plantation.

A Character of the Province of Mary-Land is not one of those "neglected classics"; first editions of the book are indeed rare. In

1939, John W. Garrett listed locations of eleven extant copies, ten in this country and one in the British Museum.[8] But since its first publication in 1666, Alsop's book has been printed five times and has been excerpted frequently in anthologies of American, writing. The first of these printings of *A Character* was edited by John Gilmary Shea and published in 1869 by William Gowans of New York as part of his Bibliotheca Americana series. Shea's edition was reprinted in 1880 at Baltimore by the Maryland Historical Society as *Fund-Publication, No. 15*. It is the Maryland Historical Society reprint that appears here in facsimile. The third printing was a new edition prepared by Newton D. Mereness and published in Cleveland in 1902. Both Shea and Mereness edited their texts from first editions, and both supplied copious notes identifying many of Alsop's allusions and supplying historical backgrounds. These three printings of the book appeared in limited editions and are themselves comparatively rare.

The fourth and fifth printing of Alsop's book was edited by Clayton Colman Hall in *Narratives of Early Maryland, 1633-1684*, first published by Charles Scribner's Sons in 1910 and reissued by Barnes and Noble in 1959. Hall also supplied notes and a brief introduction, but his text is incomplete. He omitted "certain passages" which he believed were "inserted merely for the sake of their impropriety."[9] Some of the scatological passages were deleted from Hall's text, along with the opening verses. Hall's assigning the year of composition to Alsop's letters is a valuable addition (see my "Note on the Text and the Letters" which follows).

It is beyond the scope of this facsimile reprinting to redo Shea's notes, which are often amusing, sometimes obscure, but in the main informative. Remarking on Alsop's brief treatment of the flora of Maryland, Shea writes in Note 12, "Less bombast and some details as to the botany of Maryland would have been preferable." To Alsop's statement that "he that intends to Court a *Mary-Land* Girle, must have something more than the Tautologies of a long-winded speech to carry his design," Shea speculates, "Our author evidently failed from this cause." On occasion, Shea is amusingly evasive about references to London lowlife, which

Alsop seems to have known well. Shea's notes on Whetstone's Park and Lewknor's Lane[10] are masterpieces of circumlocution at best and obscure at worst. Both places were famous for their whores—or "frail females," according to Hall's annotation.[11] Despite these problems and others, Shea's text follows closely the 1666 edition and his notes are helpful. J.A. Leo Lemay is correct, however, when he observes that "no . . . thoroughly annotated edition of Alsop's *Character* has been made."[12] That work yet remains.

Commentary on Alsop's *Character* has been relatively sparse and has appeared principally in the three introductions to the work and in anthology introductions to excerpts from the work. J.A. Leo Lemay devotes a chapter of his dissertation, "A Literary History of Colonial Maryland," to Alsop's *Character* and additional chapters to White's *Relation* and Hammond's *Leah and Rachel*. I have read the abstract of Lemay's dissertation, but out of courtesy to him have foregone the temptation of reading and summarizing his findings, which are soon to be published in book form. Lemay's "biographical appendix" on Alsop promises to add new information about this little known writer.[13]

Shea, the book's first editor, characterized Alsop's work as a "curious tract," and with this remark set the tone of much ensuing commentary. Shea regarded the book as "written in the most extravagant style" and containing "no facts as to the stirring events in Maryland history which preceded its date." The tract was "designed to stimulate emigration to Maryland, and . . . written in a vulgar style to suit the class it was to reach." Shea believed that Alsop's "portrait and his language alike bespeak the rollicking roysterer of the days of the restoration, thoroughly familiar with all the less reputable haunts of London."[14] Mereness, second editor of the book, used the word "unique" to characterize the work, adding that Alsop's description of Maryland "is decidedly the most pretentious" of the seventeenth century. For Mereness, Alsop's

little learning made him verbose, bombastic, given to ridiculous extravagance in style—even for his time—rather than refined, cultured , accurate; and his acquaintance with the disreputable places in London, together with the low moral standard of the period of the Restoration, made him vulgar rather than Puritanical in his tastes.[15]

Both Shea and Mereness agree that Alsop wrote the book to promote Lord Baltimore's colony, and believe that the proprietor himself may have paid for its publication. Both question the historical accuracy of Alsop's treatment of the indenture system, pointing out that "some conditions in this book are consequently in contrast with the real conditions for the year in which it was published."[16] Neither notes that Alsop's literacy undoubtedly made him a valuable servant to Stockett and probably mitigated the circumstances of his servitude.

Hall, third editor of the work, repeated observations made by Shea and Mereness, adding:

This author had in some way acquired a quantity of ill-assorted information, and also an extensive vocabulary, but was without sufficient education to enable him to make proper use of either. His style is therefore extravagant, inflated and grandiloquent. It is also coarse and vulgar, even for the seventeenth century.

Along with Shea and Mereness, Hall judged Alsop's narrative to be exaggerated, and like the earlier editors, Hall believed that Alsop's "story no doubt describes his own personal experiences rather than general conditions throughout the province."[17]

Following the lead of these three editors, Russel Nye and Norman Grabo described Alsop's *Character* as a "jumble of letters, descriptions of the country and its people, and absurd doggerel." They concluded that Alsop's "humorous view of the American experience finds expression in a grotesque witty style so broadly burlesque that it is often not clear whether he really means to defend Maryland or to undermine her." Darrel Abel labelled Alsop's book as a piquant but not very informative work by a "London gutter-rat with a smattering of literature and an extensive education in metropolitan low life," a man more knowledgeable about "seamy London life" than "about conditions in the

New World." The most substantial parts of the book, according
to Abel, are the sections on the Susquehannock Indians and the
tobacco trade. "Aslop has almost as much obscenity as Rabelais,
although he falls far short of him in geniality and humor," he
concluded.[18]

Moses Coit Tyler and Louis B. Wright were among the more
enthusiastic readers of Alsop's *Character*. Tyler called the book a
"jovial, vivacious, and most amusing production," whose "good
humor is of the loud-laughing kind." Alsop was a "literary merry-
andrew" and "a scaramouch with pen in hand," poking "fun at
himself as at everybody else." For Tyler, the letters were "piquant
and ridiculous," and the book itself a "medley of frolicsome
papers" and a "heterogeneous mixture of fact and fiction." He
compared Alsop's *Character* with Ward's *The Simple Cobbler of
Agawam* as one of two seventeenth century American books not-
able for "mirthful, grotesque, and slashing energy."[19]

Even more laudatory, Wright judged Alsop's *Character* "the
most vigorous and original American work of the middle decades
of the seventeenth century," a book whose "descriptions, written
in colorful and idiomatic prose, have the rhythms of the Eliza-
bethans and their zest for the world about them." Wright compared Alsop's style with that of Thomas Dekker's pamphlets and
saw Alsop as a man "of some cultivation," familiar with the works
of John Donne and others. He credited Alsop with sincerity and
truth in his descriptions, but conceded that "the book reads less
like a promotional tract than most of the descriptive works
written in the colonies."[20]

Among other commentators who have written about Alsop's
Character, Loker Raley thought the prose masculine, the descriptions lucid and terse, the poetry "not great," but "well rounded
and literary rather than inspired." Jay B. Hubbell called Alsop a
"vigorous pamphleteer" whose prose is superior to his verse, and
Harrison T. Meserole viewed the book as "an exceptionally lively
piece of writing, in part because of Alsop's keen eye for detail and
his control of prose rhythms, but also because of the author's
sharp sense of humor and uninhibited expression of opinion."

Richard Beale Davis praised *A Character* for its "frank expression
of political opinion, pungent and ribald vocabulary, and sharply
perceptive observations of colonial life." He added that "Alsop's
writing proves that the southern indentured servant might often
be a highly literate as well as highly intelligent man." And Russel
B. Nye called Alsop's effort "a strong book for strong tastes,"
"jocular, often coarse, and sometimes close to obscenity." He
also saw the satire of *A Character* as a precursor of Ebenezer
Cook's caustic account of his Maryland sojourn in *The Sot-Weed
Factor* (London, 1708).[21]

These observations represent the range of attitudes towards
Alsop and his book. While there is disagreement about the effectiveness of Alsop's language, about the character of the man
himself, and about his historical accuracy,[22] even the most critical
found the book interesting as a personal record of adventures in
the New World.

George F. Horner listed fairly specific reasons for the continu-
ing interest in Alsop's book as a colonial literary work; he suggested that Alsop's *Character* gives "evidence of more literary
pretensions" than almost any other early American writing before
it, and that "a generally comic air pervades the whole book."
He saw Alsop as "a wit, satirist, and humorist," whose book is
"crude, vulgar in many spots, but in comparison with that which
appeared before him of a much higher rank in the realm of [the]
comic." To gain these comic effects, Alsop "employs such types
of wit as the *double-entendre*, incongruous personification, extra-
vagantly extended figures of speech, and word coinages," along
with the "usual tricks of exaggeration and understatement."
Horner called Alsop's book neither a history nor a description,
but a "character." In her discussion of *A Character*, Nancy Lou
Erickson regarded Alsop as a humorist who outdistances "most, if
not all, of his predecessors in America" and the book itself as
"permeated with an incisive originality that characterizes the man
of wit."[23]

It is precisely Alsop's comic voice, wildly extravagant and
coarsely witty, and the concerns of this voice that inform *A*

Character. Alsop's exaggeration sometimes descends to nonsense, as in his digression on trade at the beginning of Chapter IV; but in the main his satire is directed at timorous Englishmen afraid to adventure and at Puritans of both Old and New Worlds,[24] not at Maryland or its inhabitants.

Alsop establishes this comic voice in the dedications and in the preface to *A Character*. To Lord Baltimore, he writes:

> If I have wrote or composed any thing that's wilde and confused, it is because I am so my self, and the world, as far as I can perceive, is not much out of the same trim; therefore I resolve, if I am brought to the Bar of *Common Law* for any thing I have done here, to plead *Non compos mentis*, to save my Bacon. (p.21)

He tells the merchant adventurers and ships' commanders, "This dish of Discourse was intended for you at first, but it was manners to let my Lord [Baltimore] have the first cut, the Pye being his own" (p. 23). To his readers, he boasts "I am so self-conceited of my own merits, that I almost think I want none," adding "I dwell so far from Neighbors, that if I do not praise my self, no body else will" (pp. 25-26). And in "The Author to His Book," Alsop burlesques the "dedicatory poem" with the following:

> When first *Apollo* got my brain with Childe,
> He made large promise never to beguile,
> But like an honest Father, he would keep
> Whatever Issue from my Brain did creep:
> With that I gave consent, and up he threw
> Me on a Bench, and strangely he did do.
>
> .　　.　　.
>
> Well, since 'tis so, I'le alter this base Fate,
> And lay his Bastard at some Noble's Gate. (p. 27)

From the beginning, Alsop's voice is that of comic braggadocio, celebrating himself and calling his book "The Bastard Off-spring of a New-born wit." The unidentified authors of the complimentary verses[25] refer specifically to the voice Alsop employs. "William Bogherst" acknowledges that

Zoilus[26] is dumb, for thou the mark hast hit,
By interlacing History with Wit. (p. 31).

Likewise, "H.W." praises Alsop for displaying Maryland's glories "in such Scenes of Witt/ That those that read must fall in Love with it." Though Alsop loses control of his language at points, *A Character* is fairly consistently sustained by a voice giving information and impressions with the comic braggadocio and coarseness frequently associated with the Southwest Humor of a century and a half later. Alsop's letters to his parents, however, show less of this braggadocio than is evident throughout the rest of the book.

Posing as "wilde and confused" and inwardly reflecting the chaos of the external world, Alsop's comic voice nevertheless assumes the existence of a definite and perceivable social order, one that has been disrupted by the Puritan Revolution. Alsop's principal concerns and the targets of his satire illustrate that his comic voice has serious, if not high, purposes.

As a Royalist, Alsop vows he would rather "serve in Chains, and draw the Plough with Animals" than submit to Oliver Cromwell and the Commonwealth rulers, whom he chastizes as traitors, "Theeves and Robbers," "barbarous Hounds," and "lustful Sodomites." Of these usurpers, he writes:

> *And that these Slaves that now predominate*
> *Hang'd and destroy'd may be their best Fate;*
> *And though Great Charles be distant from his own,*
> *Heaven I hope will seat him on his Throne.* (p. 86)

Cromwell's death is "good news," he wrote in 1658; and he hopes "the death of this great Rebel . . . will prove an *Omen* to presage the destruction of the rest." In a poem written to his brother upon receiving two caps (one plain and the other "some antient Monumental Relique") and news of the disinterrment and dessication of Cromwell's body, he observes:

> *Say, didst thou* [the fancy cap] *cover Noll's old brazen head,*
> *Which on the top of Westminster high Lead*
> *Stands on a Pole, erected to the sky,*
> *As a grand Trophy to his memory.*

From his perfidious skull didst thou fall down,
In a dis-dain to honour such a crown
With three-pile Velvet? tell me, hadst thou thy fall
From the high top of that Cathedral? (pp. 102-103)

About the Puritans of New England, he is equally vituperative:

> I must confess the *New-England* men that trade into this
> Province, had rather have fat Pork for their Goods, than
> Tobacco or Furrs, which I conceive is, because their bodies
> being fast bound up with the cords of restringent Zeal, they
> are fain to make use of the lineaments of this *Non-Canaanite*
> creature physically to loose them; for a bit of a pound upon
> a two-peny Rye loaf, according to the original Receipt, will
> bring the costiv'st red-ear'd Zealot in some three hours time
> to a fine stool, if methodically observed. (p. 69)

He makes similar observations about the Barbados traders and
about Josias Fendall, who led the so-called Fendall's Rebellion in
1660 against Lord Baltimore's agents. Fendall's is a "pigmie
Rebellion" by a company of "weak-witted men, which thought
to have traced the steps of *Oliver*." When Charles II was restored
to the throne, Alsop writes to his father, "I hope that God has
placed him there, will give him a heart to praise and magnifie his
name for ever, and a hand of just Revenge, to punish the murthering and rebellious Outrages of those Sons of shame and Apostacy,
that Usurped the Throne of his Sacred Honour" (p. 98).

Alsop couches his impressions of Maryland's countryside, inhabitants, and opportunities in hyperbole aimed at enticing and
amusing his English readers with the wonders of the New World.
A land of "natural plenty," Maryland is the "Landskip of Creation
drawn to the life," a "Terrestrial Paradice" where waterfowl
"arrive in millionous multitudes" and fish abound. The four-
legged deer of Maryland are as plentiful as the two-legged "Does
of *Whetstons* Park," and like their English counterparts "will (all
most) stand till they be scratcht." The inhabitants live in a "blessed
harmony of quietness," unharassed by the "motionated Water-
works" of lawyers' jaws, the "Aquafortial operation of great and
eating Taxes," the "Pestilential noysomness" of thieves, and the

presence of "some Night-walker, or Batchelor of Leachery, that has taken his degree three story high in a Bawdy-house." Women "are courted into a Copulative matrimony, which some of them (for aught I know) had they not come to such a Market with their Virginity, might have kept it by them untill it had been mouldy, unless they had let it out by a yearly rent to some of the Inhabitants of *Lewknors-Lane*." Men "well vers'd in the Art of perswasion" might secure the "private and reserved favour of their Mistress, if Age speak their Master deficient." Catholics and Episcopal Protestants live in harmony, but the "*Adamite, Ranter, and Fift-Monarchy men, Mary-Land* cannot, nay will not digest within her liberal stomach such corroding morsels: So that this Province is an utter Enemy to blasphemous and zealous Imprecations, drain'd from the Lymbick of hellish and damnable Spirits, as well as profuse prophaness, that issues from the prodigality of none but cract-brain Sots." Servitude, easier in Maryland than in London, is necessary because there is "no truer Emblem of Confusion, either in Monarchy or Domestick Governments, then when either Subject, or the Servant, strives for the upper hand of his Prince, or Master." Yet in Maryland, the man willing to forego "four years sordid liberty" will be provided by law with "Fifty Acres of Land, Corn to serve him a whole year, three Suits of Apparel," and tools necessary to establish himself as a Freeman, landholder, and eventually as Master.

Alsop's hyperbole is somewhat mitigated by his warnings to prospective migrants. Several times, he reminds readers of the need for "laborious industry" to survive in the New World. He says he writes of Maryland's possibilities "out of a love to my Countrymen," not to "seduce or delude any, or to draw them from their native soyle." Maryland's opportunities are many, but those

whose abilities here in *England* are capable of maintaining themselves in any reasonable and handsom manner, they had best so to remain, lest the roughness of the Ocean, together with the staring visages of the wilde Animals, which they may see after their arrival into the Country, may alter the natural dispositions of their bodies, that the stay'd and solid part that kept its motion by Doctor *Trigs* purgationary operation, may run beyond the byas of the wheel in a violent and laxative confusion. (p. 55).

For London's boastful idlers, Alsop reserves his most satiric and scatological contempt. Mere mention of the hazards of a sea voyage to them is so frightful that

> though the Port-hole of their bodies has been stopt from a convenient Evacuation some several months, theyl'e need no other Suppository to open the Orifice of their Esculent faculties then this Relation [of an ocean trip], as their Drawers or Breeches can more at large demonstrate to the inquisitive search of the curious. (p. 62)

These warnings to prospective migrants are repeatedly tinged with such coarsely playful contempt, but Alsop frequently cites the need for hard work in Maryland and directs his most satiric comments at England's poor and unemployed who are afraid of adventuring.[27]

Alsop's account of the Susquehannock Indians is one of the few contemporary records we have of this tribe which numbered about 5000 in 1600 but was extinct by 1763. Like many European and early American writers on the Indians, he provides misinformation as well as information. For example, the Susquehannocks did not have "naturally white" skin; they were not seven feet tall, according to archaeologists who have explored their burial grounds; they were not Devil worshippers. Alsop's description of this tribe as a proud and warlike people is essentially accurate, as is his account of Indian tortures and courage. When he reports that torture victims have undaunted contempt to their cruelty" and all the while sing "the summary of their Warlike Atchievements," he is perhaps alluding to the so-called death-songs or poems sung by men of some tribes at their demise. But he undercuts his portrait of the Susquehannocks by focusing his attention on their "Absurdities" and by drawing his picture "like the Painter in the Comedy, who being to limne out the Pourtraiture of the Furies, as they severally appeared, set himself behind a Pillar, and between fright and amazement, drew them by guess." Yet Alsop did have an "occular experimental view" of these Indians and does provide valuable information and impressions about them. It is interesting to note that as late as 1971, John Upton Terrell quotes Alsop on the Susquehannocks in his *American Indian Almanac.*[28]

Alsop's choice of the coarsely comic voice for his narrative separates his book from other early writing about Maryland and from most colonial American writing before the eighteenth century. Father Andrew White's *A Relation of Maryland,* written in plain and dignified prose, is a straightforward account of conditions in the colony. Unlike Alsop, White packs his *Relation* with details, shows compassion for the Indian natives, and like Captain John Smith lists the necessary provisions for those wishing to adventure.[29] In style and content, Hammond's *Leah and Rachel* stands between the accounts by White and Alsop; Hammond employs satire, but none of Alsop's bawdry. Hammond defends Virginia and Maryland against "Those blackmouthed babblers, that not only have but doe abuse so noble a plantation" and affirms life there to be easy, "yet not such a Lubberland as the Fiction of the land of Ease is reported to be, nor such a Utopian as Sr. Thomas Moore hath related to be found out." One of Hammond's purposes is to recount his role in Maryland's conflict between Puritans and Proprietary—a dispute culminating in the Battle at the Severn River on March 25, 1655, in which more than twenty men were killed, many more wounded, and four of Lord Baltimore's captured agents executed.[30] Alsop mentions nothing of these events, probably because peace was restored during his residence there and because he is more interested in conveying his impressions than in recording history. Cook's *The Sot-Weed Factor*, published more than forty years after Alsop's *Character*, employs the comic voice, engages in satire and bawdry, but makes the Marylanders the butt of his humor rather than timorous Englishmen. In the early decades of the eighteenth century, such writers as William Byrd of Westover and Robert Beverley were employing the same voice in their accounts.

Alsop's *Character* is important today as an historical document and as an unusual promotional tract. How effective such books were in promoting migration to the colonies is uncertain, for literacy was not high among members of Alsop's intended audience and the most influential means of informing Englishmen of opportunities in the New World were personal letters from actual settlers.[31] Perhaps Alsop includes his letters for this reason. For modern readers, Alsop's *Character* is chiefly significant as a literary attempt to render personal impressions of the New World in the comic mode. As a comic writer, his achievement is small, but in seventeenth century writing about colonial America, his jolly coarseness stands alone. In his use of the comic mode, the jolly coarseness of life, and the colonial American milieu, Alsop stands as the first of a line of writers which includes not only Ebenezer Cook, but also John Barth and his novelistic version of *The Sot-Weed Factor.*

Robert Bain
University of North Carolina

A NOTE ON THE TEXT AND THE LETTERS

J. A. Leo Lemay's observation that there is "no accurately printed" text of Alsop's *Character* is only partially correct. No modern edition based on collation of extant texts is available, but my comparison of Shea's text with that of the first edition in the Library of Congress shows that his edition is a faithful rendering of Alsop's book. The Library of Congress copy appears to be complete, but a few pages are partially marred so that collation is impossible. My collation showed no significant substantive variants and only a few differences in punctuation and orthography. Both Shea and Mereness mention the difficulties they faced in finding complete, unmarred editions for their texts.

A significant difference between the Shea and Mereness texts is Mereness' addition of a complimentary poem by "Will. Barber" omitted by Shea. The Library of Congress copy does not include the poem by Barber, nor does a page appear to be missing from this copy. Mereness annotates this addition as follows:

> Our knowledge of those who wrote the preceding verses to our author is confined to that gathered from this book. Those written by Will. Barber were omitted in the Gowans reprint.[33]

It is possible that the Barber poem was tipped in as an extra page in some copies after the book was printed and bound, but this problem will not be resolved until all extant copies have been collated for a modern edition. The text of the Barber poem, as printed by Mereness, appears below.

To my Friend Mr. *George Alsop*, on his *Character
of MARY-LAND.*

Columbus *with* Apollo *sure did set,
When he did Court to propigate thy Wit,
Or else thy Genius with so small a Clew,
Could not have brought such Intricates in view;
Discover'd hidden Earth so plain, that we
View more in this, then if we went to see,*
MARY-LAND, *I with some thousands more,*

Could not imagine where she stood before;
And hadst thou still been silent with thy Pen,
We had continu'd still the self-same men,
Ne're to have known the glory of that Soyle,
Whose plentious dwellings is four thousand mile.
The portly Susquehanock *in his naked dress,*
Had certain still been Pigmye, *or much less;*
All had been dark (to us) and obscure yet,
Had not thy diligence discover'd it:
For this we owe thee Praises to the Skie,
But none but MARY-LAND *can gratifie.*

Will. Barber.

Hall's dating of Alsop's letters is a valuable addition to the work. He assigns years of composition to the first eight letters with confidence; he regards his dating of the last four letters as uncertain. Below is a calendar of Hall's datings. For convenience, I have numbered the letters, listed them by the addressee, and included in parentheses the page numbers on which they begin in in the Shea text reprinted here.

1. *To my much Honored Friend* Mr. T.B. (p. 83), Aug. 19, 1658.
2. *To my Honored Father at his House* (p. 86), Sept. 6, 1658.
3. *To my Brother* (p. 88), Sept. 7, 1658.
4. *To my much Honored Friend* Mr. T.B. *at his house* (p. 90), Feb. 6, 1659.
5. *To my Father at his House* (p. 92), Jan. 17, 1659.
6. *To my much Honored Friend* Mr. M.F. (p. 95), Jan. 17, 1659.
7. *To my Honored Friend* Mr. T.B. *at his House* (p. 97), Feb. 20, 1661.
8. *To my Honored Father at his House* (p. 98), Feb. 9, 1661.
9. *To my Cosen* Mris. Ellinor Evins (p. 100), Dec. 9, 1662?
10. *To My Brother* P.A. (p. 101), Dec. 11, 1662?
11. *To my Honored Friend* Mr. T.B. (p. 105), Dec. 13, 1662?
12. *To my Parents* (p. 106), April 9, 1663?

NOTES

[1] John Gilmary Shea, ed. *A Character of the Province of Mary-Land*, by George Alsop (Baltimore, 1880), p. 88. All quotations from Alsop's *Character* are from this edition, printed in facsimile here; only the longer quotations will be noted, and these will appear in the text. References to Shea's introduction will appear in the footnotes.

[2] Ernest Bates Sutherland, "George Alsop," *Dictionary of American Biography,* I (New York, 1928), 227-228. Shea, pp. 9-10, 15. Newton D. Mereness, ed. *A Character of the Province of Mary-Land*, by George Alsop (Cleveland, 1902), pp. 7-9, 12. Clayton Colman Hall, ed. *A Character of the Province of Mary-Land*, by George Alsop in *Narratives of Early Maryland, 1633-1684* (New York, 1959). pp. 337-339.

[3] Hugh T. Lefler, "Promotional Literature of the Southern Colonies," *Journal of Southern History*, 33 (1967), 14.

[4] Howard Mumford Jones, "The Colonial Impulse: An Analysis of the 'Promotion' Literature of Colonization," *Proceedings of the American Philosophical Society*, 90 (1946), 134. Jones' essay is a comprehensive treatment of promotional writing.

[5] Lefler, p. 14.

[6] Jones, p. 133. Jones does not mention Alsop, but notes that much of Captain John Smith's writing falls into the category of "the personal report by an interested observer." Jones uses the term "personal narrative" to describe this kind of promotional writing. Alsop's use of the pronoun "I" appears, as might be expected, frequently in the letters (more than 155 times). His chapter on servitude employs the "I" some twenty times, twice as many as in the other sections.

[7] Lefler, pp. 14-15.

[8] John W. Garrett, "Seventeenth Century Books Relating to Maryland," *Maryland Historical Magazine*, 34 (1939), 27.

[9] Hall, p. 337.

[10] See Note 12, p. 111; Note 30. p. 114; and for Whetstone's

Park and Lewknor's Lane, Notes 14 and 36, 37, pp. 111, 115. For an account of London's brothels, see E. Beresford Chancellor, *The Pleasure Haunts of London during Four Centuries* (London, 1925), pp. 168-191. Chancellor also discusses other amusements.

[11] Hall, p. 346.

[12] J. A. Leo Lemay, "George Alsop" in *A Bibliographical Guide to the Study of Southern Literature*, ed. Louis D. Rubin, Jr. (Baton Rouge, 1969), p. 337.

[13] Ibid. See also J. A. Leo Lemay, "A Literary History of Colonial Maryland," *Dissertation Abstracts*, 25, 2746. Lemay completed his dissertation at the University of Pennsylvania in 1964.

[14] Shea, pp. 10-11.

[15] Mereness, pp. 5, 8.

[16] Ibid., p. 13.

[17] Hall, pp. 337, 338.

[18] Russel B. Nye and Norman S. Grabo, eds. *American Thought and Writing: The Colonial Period* (Boston, 1965), pp. 15-16. Darrel Abel, *American Literature: Colonial and Early National Writing* (Woodbury, N.Y., 1963) pp. 10-11.

[19] Moses Coit Tyler, *A History of American Literature, 1607-1765* (New York, 1962), pp. 83-86. Tyler's *History* was first published in 1878 in two volumes.

[20] Louis B. Wright, "Writers of the South" in *Literary History of the United States,* ed. Robert E. Spiller, et. al. (New York, 1953), pp. 42-43.

[21] Loker Raley, ed. *300 Years; The Poets and Poetry of Mary-Land* (New York, 1937), pp. 7-8. Jay B. Hubbell, *The South in American Literature, 1607-1900* (Duke University Press, 1954), pp. 61-62. Harrison T. Meserole, Walter Sutton, and Brom Weber, eds. *American Literature: Tradition and Innovation,*I (Lexington, Mass., 1969), pp. 27-28. Meserole assumed principal responsibility for the Colonial Period. Richard Beale Davis, C. Hugh Holman, and Louis D. Rubin, Jr., eds. *Southern Writing, 1585-1920* (New

York, 1970), pp. 40, 86. Davis edited the section dealing with Southern writing from 1585-1800. Russel B. Nye *American Literary History, 1607-1830* (New York, 1970), pp. 23-24, 99.

[22] Two writers on white servitude cite Alsop infrequently. See Abbot Emerson Smith, *Colonists in Bondage: White Servitude and Convict Labor in America, 1607-1776* (Chapel Hill, N. C., 1947). Smith cites Hammond's *Leah and Rachel* often, but refers to Alsop's account only twice (pp. 55, 255). Eugene I. MacCormac, *White Servitude in Maryland, 1634-1820* (Baltimore, Johns Hopkins Studies, 1904), pp. 48-49, 72. MacCormac says Alsop exaggerates the ease of the indenture system and that William Eddis, writing about 100 years later, is overly negative in his account of the life of Maryland servants.

[23] George F. Horner, "A History of American Humor to 1765" 2 vols. (Unpublished Doctoral Dissertation, University of North Carolina, 1938), I, 114-119. Nancy Lou Erickson, "The Early Colonial Humorist" (Unpublished Doctoral Dissertation, University of North Carolina, 1970), p. 133. Erickson devotes a whole chapter (pp. 125-161) to Alsop's *Character*; particularly interesting is her discussion of Alsop as a man of wit (pp. 154-161).

[24] Ibid., I, 116. "Lawyers, police officers, shop-keepers, timid adventurers, and democratic Puritans are singled out for his attack." To Horner's list might be added splinter religious sects (pp. 45-46, 50-51), "Batchelor[s] of Leachery" (p. 49), those who write about America without "occular and experimental views" (p. 74), those who abuse the indenture system (p. 57*ff.*), Barbados traders (pp. 69-70), "the Physical Collegians of *London*" (p. 65), etc.

[25] No editor has identified "William Bogherst" or "H. W.," authors of the complimentary verses. In *The Diary of Samuel Pepys* (IX, 201, London, 1909), editor Henry B. Wheatley mentions a "William Boghurst," author of a manuscript "Treatise on the Plague" and "apothecary, at the White Hart in St. Giles in the Fields." Boghurst advertised in the *Intelligencer* of July 31, 1665, a successful treatment for the plague. Alsop's allusions to diaphoretics, emetics, and cathartics suggest some familiarity with

the medicines of the day, but I have found no clear evidence that Wheatley's William Boghurst is the author of the complimentary verse in Alsop's *Character*. For comment on a third author of a complimentary verse, see "A Note on the Text and the Letters."

[26] Zoilus of Amphipolis was a Greek rhetorician, grammarian and critic of the 4th century B.C. He was noted for his witty and merciless attacks upon Homer's epics, upon Plato, Isocrates, and others. Bogherst evidently has in mind here Alsop's attacks on the "clappermouth jaws of the vulgar in *England*" (p. 94) who are critical of Maryland and especially the indenture system.

[27] See Jones, pp. 146-152 for a discussion of "The Population Problem and the Common Man." Though Jones focuses his remarks on the sixteenth and early seventeenth centuries, Alsop's book is concerned with what Jones calls "social dislocation" and "overpopulation."

[28] John Upton Terrell, *American Indian Almanac* (New York, 1971) pp. 183, 185. Terrell does not mention Alsop by name, only as a seventeenth century writer on the Susquehannocks. He quotes passages from pp. 72-73 of Shea's text. On the Susquehannocks, see Paul A. W. Wallace, *Indians in Pennsylvania* (Harrisburg, Pa., 1961), pp. 8-12, 95-100. Frank Webb Hodge *Handbook of American Indians North of Mexico* (Washington, D.C., 1907), II, 653-659. John R. Swanton, *The Indian Tribes of North America* (Washington, D.C., 1952), 56-57. Shea's notes on the Susquehannocks are generally accurate, but his argument that the famous Logan was a Susquehannock has not been accepted by later scholars.

[29] Father Andrew White, *A Relation of Maryland* in *Narratives of Early Maryland, 1633-1684*, ed. Clayton Colman Hall (New York, 1959), pp. 65-112.

[30] John Hammond, *Leah and Rachel, or, The Two Fruitfull Sisters Virginia and Mary-Land* in *Narratives of Early Maryland, 1633-1684*, ed. Clayton Colman Hall (New York, 1959), pp. 287, 299-300, 301-307. The number of dead and wounded varies with the different accounts of the Battle at the Severn. I have cited Hammond's account here. Other accounts of the Puritan-

Proprietary conflict in Hall's volume include: *The Lord Balte-more's Case* (London, 1653); *Virginia and Maryland, or The Lord Baltamore's Printed Case Uncased and Answered* (London, 1655); Leonard Strong, *Babylon's Fall* (London, 1655); John Langford, *Refutation of Babylon's Fall* (London, 1655).

[31] Jones, p. 131. Smith, pp. 54-57.

[32] Lemay, in *A Bibliographical Guide to the Study of Southern Literature*, p. 337.

[33] Mereness, p. 30.

ALSOP'S MARYLAND.

1 6 6 6.

REISSUED AS

𝕱und-𝕻ublication, 𝕹o. 15.

A

Character of the Province

OF

MARYLAND.

By GEORGE ALSOP.

1666.

Baltimore, 1880.

GOWANS'

BIBLIOTHECA AMERICANA.

5

"Thy fathers went down into Egypt with three score and ten persons, and now the Lord thy God hath made thee as the stars of heaven for multitude." .... *Moses.*

"Two things are to be considered in writing history, truth and elocution, for in truth consisteth the soul, and in elocution the body of history; the latter without the former, is but a picture of history; the former without the latter, unapt to instruct. The principle and proper work of history, being to instruct, and enable men by their knowledge of actions past, to bear themselves prudently in the present, and providently towards the future." .... *T. Hobbes.*

NEW YORK:

WILLIAM GOWANS.

———

1869.

64 Copies printed on large paper 4to.

A

CHARACTER OF THE PROVINCE

OF

MARYLAND.

DESCRIBED IN FOUR DISTINCT PARTS.

ALSO

**A SMALL TREATISE ON THE WILD AND NAKED INDIANS (OR
SUSQUEHANOKES) OF MARYLAND, THEIR CUSTOMS,
MANNERS, ABSURDITIES, AND RELIGION.**

TOGETHER WITH

A COLLECTION OF HISTORICAL LETTERS.

BY

GEORGE ALSOP.

**A NEW EDITION WITH AN INTRODUCTION AND COPIOUS
HISTORICAL NOTES.**

By JOHN GILMARY SHEA, LL.D.,

MEMBER OF THE NEW YORK HISTORICAL SOCIETY.

*Our western world, with all its matchless floods,
Our vast transparent lakes and boundless woods,
Stamped with the traits of majesty sublime,
Unhonored weep the silent lapse of time,
Spread their wild grandeur to the unconscious sky,
In sweetest seasons pass unheeded by;
While scarce one muse returns the songs they gave,
Or seeks to snatch their glories from the grave.*
ALEXANDER WILSON, The Ornithologist.

*The greater part of the magnificent countries east of the Alleghanies is in a high
state of cultivation and commercial prosperity, with natural advantages not sur-
passed in any country. Nature, however, still maintains her sway in some parts,
especially where pine-barrens and swamps prevail. The territory of the United
States covers an area of 2,963,666 square miles, about one-half of which is capable
of producing everything that is useful to man, but not more than a twenty-sixth
part of it has been cleared. The climate is generally healthy, the soil fertile,
abounding in mineral treasures, and it possesses every advantage from navigable
rivers and excellent harbors. ....*MRS. SOMERVILLE.

NEW YORK:

WILLIAM GOWANS.

—

1869.

5

J. MUNSELL, PRINTER,
ALBANY.

DEDICATED

TO

THE MEMORY

OF

LORD BALTIMORE.

ADVERTISEMENT.

The subscriber announces to the public, that he intends publishing a series of works, relating to the history, literature, biography, antiquities and curiosities of the Continent of America. To be entitled

GOWANS' BIBLIOTHECA AMERICANA.

The books to form this collection, will chiefly consist of reprints from old and scarce works, difficult to be produced in this country, and often also of very rare occurrence in Europe; occasionally an original work will be introduced into the series, designed to throw light upon some obscure point of American history, or to elucidate the biography of some of the distinguished men of our land. Faithful reprints of every work published will be given to the public; nothing will be added, except in the way of notes, or introduction, which will be presented entirely distinct from the body of the work. They will be brought out in the best style, both as to type, press work and paper, and in such a manner as to make them well worthy a place in any gentleman's library.

A part will appear about once in every six months, or oftener, if the public taste demand it; each part forming an entire work, either an original production, or a reprint of some valuable, and at the same time scarce tract. From eight or twelve parts will form a handsome octavo volume, which the publisher is well assured, will be esteemed entitled to a high rank in every collection of American history and literature.

Should reasonable encouragement be given, the whole collection may in the course of no long period of time become not less voluminous, and quite as valuable to the student in American history, as the celebrated Harleian Miscellany is now to the student and lover of British historical antiquities.

W. GOWANS, *Publisher.*

INTRODUCTION.

GEORGE ALSOP, the author of this curious tract, was born according to the inscription on his portrait, in 1638. He served a two years' apprenticeship to some trade in London, but seems to have been wild enough. His portrait and his language alike bespeak the rollicking roysterer of the days of the restoration, thoroughly familiar with all the less reputable haunts of London. He expresses a hearty contempt for Cromwell and his party, and it may be that the fate which confined him to a four years' servitude in Maryland was an order of transportation issued in the name of the commonwealth of England. He speaks disdainfully of the "mighty low and distracted life" of such as could not pay their passage, then, according to *Leah and Rachel* (p. 14), generally six pounds, as though want of money was not in his case the cause of his emigrating from England. He gives the letters he wrote to his family and friends on starting, but omits the date, although from allusions to the death of Cromwell in a letter dated at Gravesend, September 7th, he evidently sailed in 1658, the protector having died on the 3d of September in that year.

In Maryland he fell to the lot of Thomas Stockett, Esq., one of three brothers who came to Maryland in 1658,

perhaps at the same time as Alsop, and settled originally
it would seem in Baltimore county. It was on this estate
that Alsop spent the four years which enabled him to
write the following tract. He speaks highly of his treatment and the abundance that reigned in the Stockett
mansion.

Alsop's book appeared in 1666. One of the laudatory
verses that preface it is dated January, 1665 ($\frac{5}{6}$), and as it
would appear that he did not remain in Maryland after
the expiration of his four years, except perhaps for a short
time in consequence of a fit of sickness to which he
alludes, he probably returned to London to resume his
old career.

Of his subsequent life nothing is known, and though
Allison ascribes to him a volume of Sermons, we may
safely express our grave doubts whether the author of
this tract can be suspected of anything of the kind.

The book, written in a most extravagant style, contains
no facts as to the stirring events in Maryland history
which preceded its date, and in view, doubtless, of the
still exasperated state of public feeling, seems to have
studiously avoided all allusion to so unattractive a subject.
As an historical tract it derives its chief value from the
portion which comprises its *Relation of the Susquehanna
Indians*.

The object for which the tract was issued seems evident.
It was designed to stimulate emigration to Maryland, and
is written in a vulgar style to suit the class it was to reach.
While from its dedication to Lord Baltimore, and the
merchant adventurers, we may infer that it was paid for
by them, in order to encourage emigration, especially of
redemptioners.

Much of the early emigration to America was effected by what was called the redemption system. Under this, one disposed to emigrate, but unable to raise the £6, entered into a contract in the following form, with a merchant adventurer, ship owner or ship master, and occasionally with a gentleman emigrant of means, under which the latter gave him his passage and supplies:

The Forme of Binding a Servant.

[From *A Relation of Maryland*, &c., 1635.]

This indenture made the......day of..............in the.........yeere of our Soveraigne Lord King Charles &c betweene.............of the one party, and..............on the other party, Witnesseth that the said.............doth hereby covenant, promise and grant to and with the said.............his Executors and Assignes, to serve him from the day of the date hereof, vntill his first and next arrivall in Maryland, and after for and during the tearme of......yeeres, in such service and employment as the said..............or his assignes shall there employ him, according to the custome of the countrey in the like kind. In consideration whereof, the said..............doth promise and grant, to and with the said..............to pay for his passing and to find him with Meat, Drinke, Apparell and Lodging, with other necessaries during the said terme; and at the end of the said terme, to give him one whole yeeres provision of Corne and fifty acres of Land, according to the order of the countrey. In witnesse whereof, the said..............hath hereunto put his hand and seale the day and yeere above written.

Sealed and delivered }
   in the presence of }

The term of service, at first limited to five years (*Relation of Maryland*, 1635, p. 63), was subsequently reduced to four (Act of 1638, &c.), and so remained into the next century (Act of April, 1715). Thus a woman in the *Sot Weed Factor*, after speaking of her life in England, says:

> Not then a slave for twice two year,
> My cloaths were fashionably new,
> Nor were my shifts of linnen Blue;
> But things are changed; now at the Hoe,
> I daily work and Barefoot go,
> In weeding Corn or feeding Swine,
> I spend my melancholy Time.

Disputes arose as to the time when the term began, and it was finally fixed at the anchoring of the vessel in the province, but not more than fourteen days were to be allowed for anchoring after they passed the Capes (Act of 1715). When these agreements were made with the merchant adventurer, ship owner or ship captain, the servants were sold at auctions, which were conducted on the principle of our tax sales, the condition being the payment of the advances, and the bidding being for the term of service, descending from the legal limit according to his supposed value as a mechanic or hand, the best man being taken for the shortest term. Where the emigrants made their agreement with the gentleman emigrant, they proceeded at once to the land he took up, and in the name of the servant the planter took up at least one hundred acres of land, fifty of which, under the agreement, he conveyed to the servant at the expiration of his term of service.

Alsop seems to have made an agreement, perhaps on the voyage, with Thomas Stockett, Esq., as his first letter from America mentions his being in the service of that gentleman. His last letter is dated at Gravesend, the 7th of September, and his first in Maryland January 17 (1659), making a voyage of four months, which he loosely calls five, and describes as "a blowing and dangerous passage."

Through the kindness of George Lynn Lachlin Davis, Esq., I have been enabled to obtain from J. Shaaf Stockett, Esq., a descendant of Captain Stockett, some details as to his ancestor, the master of our author, during his four years' servitude, which was not very grievous to him, for he says, "had I known my yoak would have been so easie (as I conceive it will) I would have been here long before now, rather than to have dwelt under the pressure of a Rebellious and Trayterous government so long as I did."

A manuscript statement made some years later by one Joseph Tilly, states: "About or in y° year of o^r Lord 1667 or 8 I became acquainted wth 4 Gent^n y^t were brethren & then dwellers here in Maryland the elder of them went by y° name of Coll° Lewis Stockett & y° second by y° name of Captn Thomas Stockett, y° third was Doct^r Francis Stockett & y° Fourth Brother was Mr Henry Stockett. These men were but y^n newly seated or seating in Anne Arunndell County & they had much business w^h the Lord Baltimore then pp^{etor} of y° Provinces, my house standing convenient they were often entertained there: they told mee y^t they were Kentish men or Men of Kent & y^t for that they had been concerned for King Charles y° first, were out of favour wth y° following Governm^t they Mortgaged a Good an estate to follow King Charles the second in his exile & at their Return they had not money to redeem their mortgage, wch was y° cause of their coming hither.   Joseph Tilly."

Of the brothers, who are said to have arrived in the spring or summer of 1658, only Captain Thomas Stockett remained in Maryland, the others having, according to family tradition, returned to England. As stated in the document just given, they settled in Anne Arundell county, and on the 19th of July, 1669, "Obligation," a tract of 664 acres of land was patented to Captain Thomas Stockett, and a part still after the lapse of nearly two centuries remains in the family, being owned by Frank H. Stockett, Esq., of the Annapolis bar.

By his wife Mary (*Wells* it is supposed), Captain Thomas Stockett had one son, Thomas, born April 17, 1667, from whose marriage with Mary, daughter of Thomas Sprigg, of West River, gentleman (March 12, 1689), and subsequent marriage with Damarris Welch, the Stocketts of Maryland, Kentucky, Pennsylvania, New York and New Jersey are descended.

The arms of this branch, as given in the family archives, are " Or a Lyon rampant sable armed and Langued Gules a cheife of ye second a castle Tripple towred argent betwixt two Beausants — to ye crest upon a helm on a wreath of ye colours, a Lyon Proper segeant supporte on a stock ragged and trunked argent Borne by the name of Stockett with a mantle Gules doubled Argent." These agree with the arms given by Burke as the arms of the Stocketts of St. Stephens, county of Kent.

Thomas Stockett's will, dated April 23, 1671, was proved on the 4th of May in the same year, so that his death must have occurred within the ten intervening days. He left his estate to his wife for life, then his lands to his son Thomas, and his posthumous child if a son, and his personal estate to be divided among his daughters. His executors were his brothers Francis and Henry and his brother (in-law) Richard Wells. His dispositions of property are brief, much of the will consisting of pious expressions and wishes.

To return to the early Maryland emigration, at the time there was evident need for some popular tract to remove a prejudice that had been created against that colony, especially in regard to the redemptioners. The condition of those held for service in Maryland had been represented as pitiable indeed, the labor intolerable, the usage bad, the diet hard, and that no beds were allowed but the bare boards. Such calumnies had already been refuted in 1656 by Hammond, in his *Leah and Rachel.* Yet it would seem that ten years later the proprietor of Maryland found it necessary to give Alsop's flattering picture as a new antidote.

The original tract is reproduced so nearly in fac simile here that little need be said about it. The original is a very small volume, the printed matter on the page being only $2\frac{1}{8}$ inches by $4\frac{7}{8}$. (See note No. 1).

At the end are two pages of advertisements headed "These Books, with others, are Printed for Peter Dring, and are to be sold at his Shop, at the Sun in the Poultrey, next door to the Rose Tavern."

Among the books are Eliana, Holesworth's Valley of Vision, Robotham's Exposition of Solomon's Song, N. Byfields' Marrow of the Oracle of God, Pheteplace's Scrutinia Sacra, Featly Tears in Time of Pestilence, Templum Musicum by Joannes Henricus Alstedius, two cook books, a jest book, Troads Englished, and ends with A Comment upon the Two Tales of our Renowned Poet Sir Jeffray Chaucer, Knight.

At the end of this is the following by way of erratum: "Courteous Reader. In the first Epistle Dedicatory, for Felton read Feltham."

View here the Shadow whose Ingenious Hand
Hath drawne exact the Province Mary Land
Display'd her Glory in such Scænes of Witt
That those that read must fall in Love with it
For which his Labour hee deserves the praise
As well as Poets doe the wreath of Bays .

Anno Dō: 1666. Ætatis Suæ 28 .   H.W.

A

CHARACTER

Of the PROVINCE of

MARY-LAND,

Wherein is Defcribed in four diftinct
Parts, (*Viz.*)

I. *The Scituation, and plenty of the Province.*

II. *The Laws, Cuftoms, and natural Demeanor of the Inhabitant.*

III. *The worft and beft Vfage of a Mary-
Land Servant, opened in view.*

IV. *The Traffique, and Vendable Commodities
of the Countrey.*

ALSO

𝕬 **fmall** *Treatife* on the Wilde and
Naked INDIANS (or *Sufquehanokes*)
of *Mary-Land*, their Cuftoms, Manners, Abfurdities, & Religion.

Together with a Collection of Hifto-
rical LETTERS.

By GEORGE ALSOP.

London, Printed by *T. J.* for *Peter Dring*,
at the fign of the Sun in the *Poultrey;* 1666.

3

CÆCILIUS LORD BALTEMORE, (see note No. 2)

Absolute Lord and Proprietary of the Provinces of *Mary-Land* and *Avalon* (see note No. 3) in *America.*

MY LORD,

I Have adventured on your Lordships acceptance by guess; if presumption has led me into an Error that deserves correction, I heartily beg Indempnity, and resolve to repent soundly for it, and do so no more. What I present I know to be true, Experientia docet; It being an infallible Maxim, *That there is no Globe like the occular and experimental view of a Countrey.* And had not Fate by a necessary imployment, consin'd me within the narrow walks of a four years Servitude, and by degrees led me through the most intricate and dubious paths of this Countrey, by a commanding and undeniable Enjoyment, I could not, nor should I ever have undertaken to have written a line of this nature.

THE EPISTLE DEDICATORY.

If I have wrote or composed any thing that's wilde and confused, it is because I am so my self, and the world, as far as I can perceive, is not much out of the same trim; therefore I resolve, if I am brought to the Bar of *Common Law* for any thing I have done here, to plead *Non compos mentis*, to save my Bacon.

There is an old Saying in English, *He must rise betimes that would please every one.* And I am afraid I have lain so long a bed, that I think I shall please no body; if it must be so, I cannot help it. But as *Feltham* (see note No. 4) in his *Resolves* says, *In things that must be, 'tis good to be resolute;* And therefore what Destiny has ordained, I am resolved to wink, and stand to it. So leaving your Honour to more serious meditations, I subscribe my self,

      My Lord
            Your Lordship most
                Humble Servant,
                    GEORGE ALSOP.

To all the Merchant Adventurers for MARY-LAND,
together with those Commanders of Ships
that saile into that Province.

SIRS,

Y ou *are both Adventurers, the one of Estate, the
other of Life: I could tell you I am an Adventurer too, if I durst presume to come into your Company.
I have ventured to come abroad in Print, and if I should
be laughed at for my good meaning, it would so break
the credit of my understanding, that I should never dare
to shew my face upon the Exchange of (conceited) Wits
again.*

*This dish of Discourse was intended for you at first,
but it was manners to let my Lord have the first cut, the
Pye being his own. I beseech you accept of the matter
as 'tis drest, only to stay your stomachs, and I'le promise
you the next shall be better done, 'Tis all as I can serve
you in at present, and it may be questionable whether I
have served you in this or no. Here I present you with*
A Character of Mary-Land, *it may be you will say 'tis
weakly done, if you do I cannot help it, 'tis as well as I
could do it, considering several Obstacles that like blocks
were thrown in my way to hinder my proceeding: The
major part thereof was written in the intermitting time
of my sickness, therefore I hope the afflicting weakness of*

431

my Microcosm may plead a just excuse for some imperfections of my pen. I protest what I have writ is from
an experimental knowledge of the Country, and not from
any imaginary supposition. If I am blamed for what I
have done too much, it is the first, and I will irrevocably
promise it shall be the last. There's a Maxim upon
Tryals at Assizes, That if a thief be taken upon the first
fault, if it be not to hainous, they only burn him in the
hand and let him go (see note No. 5): So I desire you
to do by me, if you find any thing that bears a criminal
absurdity in it, only burn me for my first fact and let
me go. But I am affraid I have kept you too long in
the Entry, I shall desire you therefore to come in and
sit down.

G. ALSOP.

PREFACE

READER.

The Reason why I appear in this place is, lest the general Reader should conclude I have nothing to say for my self; and truly he's in the right on't, for I have but little to say (for my self) at this time: For I have had so large a Journey, and so heavy a Burden to bring *Mary-Land* into *England*, that I am almost out of breath: I'le promise you after I am come to my self, you shall hear more of me. Good Reader, because you see me make a brief Apologetical excuse for my self, don't judge me; for I am so self-conceited of my own merits, that I almost think I want none. *De Lege non judicandum ex solâ linea,* saith the Civilian; We must not pass judgement upon a Law by one line: And because we see but a small Bush at a Tavern door, conclude there is no Canary (see note No. 6). For as in our vulgar Resolves 'tis said, *A good face needs no Band, and an ill one deserves none:* So the French Proverb sayes, Bon Vien il n'a faut point de Ensigne, Good Wine needs no Bush. I suppose by this time some of my speculative observers

4

have judged me vainglorious; but if they did but rightly consider me, they would not be so censorious. For I dwell so far from Neighbors, that if I do not praise my self, no body else will: And since I am left alone, I am resolved to summon the *Magna Charta* of Fowles to the Bar for my excuse, and by their irrevocable Statutes plead my discharge. *For its an ill Bird will befoule her own Nest:* Besides, I have a thousand *Billings-gate* (see note No. 7) Collegians that will give in their testimony, *That they never knew a Fish-woman cry stinking Fish.* Thus leaving the Nostrils of the Citizens Wives to demonstrate what they please as to that, and thee (Good Reader) to say what thou wilt, I bid thee Farewel.

GEO. ALSOP.

A U T H O R

B O O K .

When first *Apollo* got my brain with Childe,
    He made large promise never to beguile,
But like an honest Father, he would keep
Whatever Issue from my Brain did creep:
With that I gave consent, and up he threw
Me on a Bench, and strangely he did do;
Then every week he daily came to see
How his new Physick still did work with me.
And when he did perceive he'd don the feat,
Like an unworthy man he made retreat,
Left me in desolation, and where none
Compassionated when they heard me groan.
What could he judge the Parish then would think,
To see me fair, his Brat as black as Ink?
If they had eyes, they'd swear I were no Nun,
But got with Child by some black *Africk* Son,
And so condemn me for my Fornication,
To beat them Hemp to stifle half the Nation.
Well, since 'tis so, I'le alter this base Fate,
And lay his Bastard at some Noble's Gate;
Withdraw my self from Beadles, and from such,
Who would give twelve pence I were in their clutch:

Then, who can tell? this Child which I do hide,
May be in time a Small-beer Col'nel *Pride* (see note
But while I talk, my business it is dumb,   [No. 8).
I must lay double-clothes unto thy Bum,
Then lap thee warm, and to the world commit
The Bastard Off-spring of a New-born wit.
Farewel, poor Brat, thou in a monstrous World,
In swadling bands, thus up and down art hurl'd;
There to receive what Destiny doth contrive,
Either to perish, or be sav'd alive.
Good Fate protect thee from a Criticks power,
For If he comes, thou'rt gone in half an hour,
Stiff'd and blasted, 'tis their usual way,
To make that Night, which is as bright as Day.
For if they once but wring, and skrew their mouth,
Cock up their Hats, and set the point Du-South,
Armes all a kimbo, and with belly strut,
As if they had *Parnassus* in their gut:
These are the Symtomes of the murthering fall
Of my poor Infant, and his burial.
Say he should miss thee, and some ign'rant Asse
Should find thee out, as he along doth pass,
It were all one, he'd look into thy Tayle,
To see if thou wert Feminine or Male ;
When he'd half starv'd thee, for to satisfie
His peeping Ign'rance, he'd then let thee lie ;
And vow by's wit he ne're could understand,
The Heathen dresses of another Land :
Well, 'tis no matter, wherever such as he
Knows one grain, more than his simplicity.
Now, how the pulses of my senses beat,
To think the rigid Fortune thou wilt meet;

Asses and captious Fools, not six in ten
Of thy Spectators will be real men,
To Umpire up the badness of the cause,
And screen my weakness from the rav'nous Laws,
Of those that will undoubted sit to see
How they might blast this new-born Infancy:
If they should burn him, they'd conclude hereafter,
'Twere too good death for him to dye a Martyr;
And if they let him live, they think it will
Be but a means for to encourage ill,
And bring in time some strange *Antipod'ans*,
A thousand Leagues beyond *Philippians*,
To storm our Wits; therefore he must not rest,
But shall be hang'd, for all he has been prest:
Thus they conclude. — My Genius comforts give,
In Resurrection he will surely live.

To my Friend Mr. GEORGE ALSOP, on his Character of MARY-LAND.

WHo such odd nookes of Earths great mass describe,
    Prove their descent from old Columbus tribe:
Some Boding augur did his Name devise,
Thy Genius too cast in th' same mould and size;
His Name predicted he would be a Rover,
And hidden places of this Orb discover;
He made relation of that World in gross,
Thou the particulars retail'st to us:
By this first Peny of thy fancy we
Discover what thy greater Coines will be;
This Embryo thus well polisht doth presage,
The manly Atchievements of its future age.
Auspicious winds blow gently on this spark,
Untill its flames discover what's yet dark;
Mean while this short Abridgement we embrace,
Expecting that thy busy soul will trace
Some Mines at last which may enrich the World,
And all that poverty may be in oblivion hurl'd.
Zoilus is dumb, for thou the mark hast hit,
By interlacing History with Wit:
Thou hast described its superficial Treasure,
Anatomiz'd its bowels at thy leasure;
That MARY-LAND to thee may duty owe,
Who to the World dost all her Glory shew,
Then thou shalt make the Prophesie fall true,
Who fill'st the World (like th' Sea) with knowledge new.

               WILLIAM BOGHERST. (See note No. 9.)

To my Friend Mr. GEORGE ALSOP, on his Character of
MARY-LAND.

THis *plain, yet pithy and concise Description*
  Of Mary-Lands *plentious and sedate condition,*
With other things herein by you set forth,
To shew its Rareness, and declare its Worth ;
Compos'd in such a time, when most men were
Smitten with Sickness, or surpriz'd with Fear,
Argues a Genius good, and Courage stout,
In bringing this Design so well about :
Such generous Freedom waited on thy brain,
The Work was done in midst of greatest pain ;
And matters flow'd so swiftly from thy source,
Nature design'd thee (sure) for such Discourse.
Go on then with thy Work so well begun,
Let it come forth, and boldly see the Sun ;
Then shall't be known to all, that from thy Youth
Thou heldst it Noble to maintain the Truth,
'Gainst all the Rabble-rout, that yelping stand,
To cast aspersions on thy MARY-LAND :
But this thy Work shall vindicate its Fame,
And as a Trophy memorize thy Name,
So if without a Tomb thou buried be,
This Book's a lasting Monument for thee.
          H. W., Master of Arts. (See note No. 10).

From my Study,
  Jan. 10, 1665.

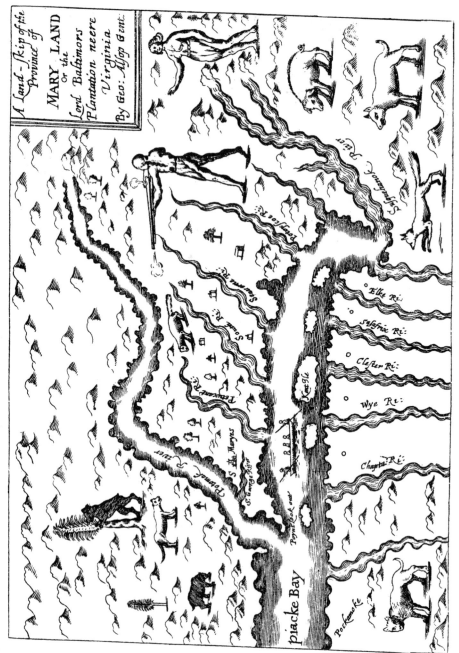

A Land-Skip of the
Province of
MARY LAND
or the
Lord Baltemors
Plantation neere
Virginia
By Geo: Alsop Gent:

Sufquahanock River

Dragon Ri:

Shaw Ri:

South Ri:

Patuxent Ri:

Elke Ri:

Sasafrix Ri:

Chester Ri:

Wye Ri:

Chaptni Ri:

Kent Ifle

St: Maryes

St: George River

S: Thomas River

Pyms Pook cut

Piacke Bay

Pockomoke

A

CHARACTER

MARY-LAND.

CHAP. I.

Of the situation and plenty of the Province of Mary-Land.

MARY-LAND is a Province situated upon the large extending bowels of *America,* under the Government of the Lord *Baltemore,* adjacent Northwardly upon the Confines of *New-England,* and neighbouring Southwardly upon *Virginia,* dwelling pleasantly upon the Bay of *Chœsapike* (see note No. 11), between the Degrees of 36 and 38, in the Zone temperate, and by Mathematical computation is eleven hundred and odd Leagues in Longitude from *England,* being within her own imbraces extraordinary pleasant and fertile. Pleasant, in respect of the multitude of Navigable Rivers and Creeks that conveniently and most profitably lodge within the armes of her green, spreading, and delightful Woods; whose natural womb (by her plenty) maintains and preserves the several diversities of Animals that rangingly inhabit her Woods; as she doth otherwise generously fructifie this piece of Earth with almost all sorts of Vegetables, as well Flowers with their varieties of colours and smells, as Herbes and Roots with their several effects and operative virtues, that offer their benefits daily to supply the want of the Inhabitant whene're their necessities shall *Sub-pœna* them to wait on their commands. So that he, who out of curiosity desires to see the Landskip of the Creation drawn to the life, or to read Natures universal Herbal without book, may with the Opticks of a discreet discerning, view *Mary-Land* drest in her green and fragrant Mantle of the Spring. Neither do I think there is any place under the Heavenly altitude, or that has footing or room upon the circular Globe of this world, that can parallel this fertile and pleasant piece of ground in its multiplicity, or rather Natures extravagancy of a superabounding plenty. For so much doth this Country increase in a swelling Spring-tide of rich variety and diversities of all things, not only common provisions that supply the reaching stomach of man with a satisfactory plenty, but also extends with its liberality and free convenient benefits to each sensitive faculty, according to their several desiring Appetites. So that had Nature made it her business, on purpose to have found out a situation for the Soul of profitable Ingenuity, she could not have fitted herself better in the traverse of the whole Universe, nor in convenienter terms have told man, *Dwell here, live plentifully and be rich.*

The Trees, Plants, Fruits, Flowers, and Roots that grow here in *Mary-Land*, are the only Emblems or Hieroglyphicks of our Adamitical or Primitive situation, as well for their variety as odoriferous smells, together with their vertues, according to their several effects, kinds and properties, which still bear the Effigies of Innocency according to their original Grafts; which by their dumb vegetable Oratory, each hour speaks to the Inhabitant in silent acts, That they need not look for any other Terrestrial Paradice, to suspend or tyre their curiosity upon, while she is extant. For within her doth dwell so much of variety, so much of natural plenty, that there is not any thing that is or may be rare, but it inhabits within this plentious soyle: So that those parts of the Creation that have borne the Bell away (for many ages) for a vegetable plentiousness, must now in silence strike and vayle all, and whisper softly in the auditual parts of *Mary-Land*, that *None but she in this dwells singular;* and that as well for that she doth exceed in those Fruits, Plants, Trees and Roots, that dwell and grow in their several Clymes or habitable parts of the Earth besides, as the rareness and super-excellency of her own glory, which she flourishly abounds in, by the abundancy of reserved Rarities, such as the remainder of the World (with all its speculative art) never bore any occular testimony of as yet. I shall forbear to particularize those several sorts of vegetables that flourishingly grows here, by

reason of the vast tediousness that will attend upon
the description, which therefore makes them much
more fit for an Herbal, than a small Manuscript or
History. (See note No. 12).

As for the wilde Animals of this Country, which
loosely inhabits the Woods in multitudes, it is impossible to give you an exact description of them all,
considering the multiplicity as well as the diversity of
so numerous an extent of Creatures : But such as has
fallen within the compass or prospect of my knowledge,
those you shall know of; *videlicet*, the Deer, because
they are oftner seen, and more participated of by the
Inhabitants of the Land, whose acquaintance by a
customary familiarity becomes much more common
than the rest of Beasts that inhabit the Woods by
using themselves in Herds about the Christian Plantations. Their flesh, which in some places of this
Province is the common provision the Inhabitants
feed on, and which through the extreme glut and
plenty of it, being daily killed by the *Indians*, and
brought in to the *English*, as well as that which is
killed by the Christian Inhabitant, that doth it more
for recreation, than for the benefit they reap by it.
I say, the flesh of Venison becomes (as to food) rather
denyed, than any way esteemed or desired.   And this
I speak from an experimental knowledge ; For when
I was under a Command, and debarr'd of a four years
ranging Liberty in the Province of *Mary-Land*, the
Gentleman whom I served my conditional and pre-

fixed time withall, had at one time in his house four-
score Venisons, besides plenty of other provisions to
serve his Family nine months, they being but seven
in number; so that before this Venison was brought
to a period by eating, it so nauseated our appetites
and stomachs, that plain bread was rather courted
and desired than it.

The Deer (see note No. 13) here neither in shape
nor action differ from our Deer in *England :* the Park
they traverse their ranging and unmeasured walks in,
is bounded and impanell'd in with no other pales than
the rough and billowed Ocean : They are also mighty
numerous in the Woods, and are little or not at all
affrighted at the face of a man, but (like the Does of
Whetstons Park) (see note No. 14) though their hydes
are not altogether so gaudy to extract an admiration
from the beholder, yet they will stand (all most) till
they be scratcht.

As for the Wolves, Bears, and Panthers (see note
No. 15) of this Country, they inhabit commonly in
great multitudes up in the remotest parts of the Continent; yet at some certain time they come down
near the Plantations, but do little hurt or injury
worth noting, and that which they do is of so degenerate and low a nature, (as in reference to the fierceness
and heroick vigour that dwell in the same kind of
Beasts in other Countries), that they are hardly worth
mentioning : For the highest of their designs and
circumventing reaches is but cowardly and base, only

to steal a poor Pigg, or kill a lost and half starved
Calf. The Effigies of a man terrifies them dreadfully,
for they no sooner espy him but their hearts are at
their mouths, and the spurs upon their heels, they
(having no more manners than Beasts) gallop away,
and never bid them farewell that are behind them.

The Elke, the Cat of the Mountain, the Rackoon,
the Fox, the Beaver, the Otter, the Possum, the Hare,
the Squirril, the Monack, the Musk-Rat (see note
No. 16), and several others (whom I'le omit for
brevity sake) inhabit here in *Mary-Land* in several
droves and troops, ranging the Woods at their
pleasure.

The meat of most of these Creatures is good for
eating, yet of no value nor esteem here, by reason of
the great plenty of other provisions, and are only
kill'd by the *Indians* of the Country for their Hydes
and Furrs, which become very profitable to those that
have the right way of traffiquing for them, as well as
it redounds to the *Indians* that take the pains to catch
them, and to slay and dress their several Hydes,
selling and disposing them for such commodities as
their Heathenish fancy delights in.

As for those Beasts that were carried over at the
first seating of the Country, to stock and increase the
situation, as Cows, Horses, Sheep and Hogs (see note
No. 17), they are generally tame, and use near home,
especially the Cows, Sheep and Horses. The Hogs,
whose increase is innumerable in the Woods, do dis-

frequent home more than the rest of Creatures that are look'd upon as tame, yet with little trouble and pains they are slain and made provision of. Now they that will with a right Historical Survey, view the Woods of *Mary-Land* in this particular, as in reference to Swine, must upon necessity judge this Land lineally descended from the *Gadarean* Territories. (See note No. 18.)

Mary-Land (I must confess) cannot boast of her plenty of Sheep here, as other Countries; not but that they will thrive and increase here, as well as in any place of the World besides, but few desire them, because they commonly draw down the Wolves among the Plantations, as well by the sweetness of their flesh, as by the humility of their nature, in not making a defensive resistance against the rough dealing of a ravenous Enemy. They who for curiosity will keep Sheep, may expect that after the Wolves have breathed themselves all day in the Woods to sharpen their stomachs, they will come without fail and sup with them at night, though many times they surfeit themselves with the sawce that's dish'd out of the muzzle of a Gun, and so in the midst of their banquet (poor Animals) they often sleep with their Ancestors.

Fowls of all sorts and varieties dwell at their several times and seasons here in *Mary-Land*. The Turkey, the Woodcock, the Pheasant, the Partrich, the Pigeon, and others, especially the Turkey, whom I have seen

6   449

in whole hundreds in flights in the Woods of *Mary-Land*, being an extraordinary fat Fowl, whose flesh is very pleasant and sweet. These Fowls that I have named are intayled from generation to generation to the Woods. The Swans, the Geese and Ducks (with other Water-Fowl) derogate in this point of setled residence; for they arrive in millionous multitudes in *Mary-Land* about the middle of *September*, and take their winged farewell about the midst of *March* (see note No. 19) : But while they do remain, and beleagure the borders of the shoar with their winged Dragoons, several of them are summoned by a Writ of *Fieri facias,* to answer their presumptuous contempt upon a Spit.

As for Fish, which dwell in the watry tenements of the deep, and by a providential greatness of power, is kept for the relief of several Countries in the world (which would else sink under the rigid enemy of want), here in *Mary-Land* is a large sufficiency, and plenty of almost all sorts of Fishes, which live and inhabit within her several Rivers and Creeks, far beyond the apprehending or crediting of those that never saw the same, which with very much ease is catched, to the great refreshment of the Inhabitants of the Province.

All sorts of Grain, as Wheat, Rye, Barley, Oates, Pease, besides several others that have their original and birth from the fertile womb of this Land (and no where else), they all grow, increase, and thrive here in *Mary-Land,* without the chargable and laborious manuring of the Land with Dung; increasing in such a measure and plenty, by the natural richness of the Earth, with the common, beneficial and convenient showers of rain that usually wait upon the several Fields of Grain (by a natural instinct), so that Famine (the dreadful Ghost of penury and want) is never known with his pale visage to haunt the Dominions of *Mary-Land.*   (See note No. 20).

> *Could'st thou (O Earth) live thus obscure, and now*
> *Within an Age, shew forth thy plentious brow*
> *Of rich variety, gilded with fruitful Fame,*
> *That (Trumpet-like) doth Heraldize thy Name,*
> *And tells the World there is a Land now found,*
> *That all Earth's Globe can't parallel its Ground ?*
> *Dwell, and be prosperous, and with thy plenty feed*
> *The craving Carkesses of those Souls that need.*

CHAP. II.

Of the Government and Natural Disposition of the People.

MARY-LAND, not from the remoteness of her situation, but from the regularity of her well ordered Government, may (without sin, I think) be called *Singular:* And though she is not supported with such large Revenues as some of her Neighbours are, yet such is her wisdom in a reserved silence, and not in pomp, to shew her well-conditioned Estate, in relieving at a distance the proud poverty of those that wont be seen they want, as well as those which by undeniable necessities are drove upon the Rocks of pinching wants: Yet such a loathsome creature is a common and folding-handed Beggar, that upon the penalty of almost a perpetual working in Imprisonment, they are not to appear, nor lurk near our vigilant and laborious dwellings. The Country hath received a general spleen and antipathy against the very name and nature of it; and though there were no Law provided (as there is) to suppress it, I am certainly confident, there is none within the Province that would lower themselves so much below the dignity of men to beg, as long as limbs and life keep house together; so much is a vigilant industrious care esteem'd.

He that desires to see the real Platform of a quiet and sober Government extant, Superiority with a meek and yet commanding power sitting at the Helme, steering the actions of State quietly, through the multitude and diversity of Opinionous waves that diversly meet, let him look on *Mary-Land* with eyes admiring, and he'll then judge her, *The Miracle of this Age.*

Here the *Roman Catholick*, and the *Protestant Episcopal* (whom the world would perswade have proclaimed open Wars irrevocably against each other), contrarywise concur in an unanimous parallel of friendship, and inseparable love intayled into one another: All Inquisitions, Martyrdom, and Banishments are not so much as named, but unexpressably abhorr'd by each other.

The several Opinions and Sects that lodge within this Government, meet not together in mutinous contempts to disquiet the power that bears Rule, but with a reverend quietness obeys the legal commands of Authority. (See note No. 21). Here's never seen Five Monarchies in a Zealous Rebellion, opposing the Rights and Liberties of a true setled Government, or Monarchical Authority: Nor did I ever see (here in *Mary-Land*) any of those dancing Adamitical Sisters, that plead a primitive Innocency for their base obscenity, and naked deportment; but I conceive if some of them were there at some certain time of the year, between the Months of *January* and *February*,

when the winds blow from the North-West quarter of
the world, that it would both cool, and (I believe)
convert the hottest of these Zealots from their burning and fiercest concupiscence. (See note No. 22).

The Government of this Province doth continually,
by all lawful means, strive to purge her Dominions
from such base corroding humors, that would predominate upon the least smile of Liberty, did not the Laws
check and bridle in those unwarranted and tumultuous
Opinions. And truly, where a kingdom, State or
Government, keeps or cuts down the weeds of destruc-
tive Opinions, there must certainly be a blessed harmony of quietness. And I really believe this Land or
Government of *Mary-Land* may boast, that she enjoys
as much quietness from the disturbance of Rebellious
Opinions, as most States or Kingdoms do in the
world : For here every man lives quietly, and follows
his labour and imployment desiredly; and by the
protection of the Laws, they are supported from those
molestious troubles that ever attend upon the Com-
mons of other States and Kingdoms, as well as from
the Aquafortial operation of great and eating Taxes.
Here's nothing to be levyed out of the Granaries of
Corn; but contrarywise, by a Law every Domestick
Governor of a Family is enjoyned to make or cause
to be made so much Corn by a just limitation, as shall
be sufficient for him and his Family (see note No. 23):
So that by this wise and *Janus*-like providence, the
thin-jawed Skeliton with his starv'd Carkess is never

seen walking the Woods of *Mary-Land* to affrighten
Children.

Once every year within this Province is an Assembly called, and out of every respective County (by the
consent of the people) there is chosen a number of
men, and to them is deliver'd up the Grievances of the
Country; and they maturely debate the matters, and
according to their Consciences make Laws for the
general good of the people; and where any former
Law that was made, seems and is prejudicial to the
good or quietness of the Land, it is repeal'd.   These
men that determine on these matters for the Repub-
lique, are called Burgesses, and they commonly sit in
Junto about six weeks, being for the most part good
ordinary Householders of the several Counties, which
do more by a plain and honest Conscience, than by
artificial Syllogisms drest up in gilded Orations. (See
note No. 24).

Here Suits and Tryals in Law seldome hold dispute
two Terms or Courts, but according as the Equity of
the Cause appears is brought to a period. (See note
No. 25).   The *Temples* and *Grays-Inne* are clear out
of fashion here: Marriot (see note No. 26) would
sooner get a paunch-devouring meal for nothing, than
for his invading Counsil.   Here if the Lawyer had
nothing else to maintain him but his bawling, he
might button up his Chops, and burn his Buckrom
Bag, or else hang it upon a pin untill its Antiquity
had eaten it up with durt and dust: Then with a

Spade, like his Grandsire *Adam,* turn up the face of
the Creation, purchasing his bread by the sweat of his
brows, that before was got by the motionated Water-
works of his jaws. So contrary to the Genius of the
people, if not to the quiet Government of the Province,
that the turbulent Spirit of continued and vexatious
Law, with all its querks and evasions, is openly and
most eagerly opposed, that might make matters either
dubious, tedious, or troublesom. All other matters
that would be ranging in contrary and improper
Spheres, (in short) are here by the Power moderated,
lower'd and subdued. All villanous Outrages that
are committed in other States, are not so much as
known here: A man may walk in the open Woods
as secure from being externally dissected, as in his
own house or dwelling. So hateful is a Robber, that
if but once imagin'd to be so, he's kept at a distance,
and shun'd as the Pestilential noysomness. (See note
No. 27).

It is generally and very remarkably observed, That
those whose Lives and Conversations have had no
other gloss nor glory stampt on them in their own
Country, but the stigmatization of baseness, were here
(by the common civilities and deportments of the
Inhabitants of this Province) brought to detest and
loath their former actions. Here the Constable hath
no need of a train of Holberteers (see note No. 28),
that carry more Armour about them, than heart to
guard him: Nor is he ever troubled to leave his

Feathered Nest to some friendly successor, while he
is placing of his Lanthern-horn Guard at the end of
some suspicious Street, to catch some Night-walker,
or Batchelor of Leachery, that has taken his Degree
three story high in a Bawdy-house. Here's no *New-
gates* for pilfering Felons, nor *Ludgates* for Debtors,
nor any *Bridewels* (see note No. 29) to lash the soul
of Concupiscence into a chast Repentance. For as
there is none of these Prisons in *Mary-Land*, so the
merits of the Country deserves none, but if any be
foully vitious, he is so reserv'd in it, that he seldom
or never becomes popular. Common Alehouses (whose
dwellings are the only Receptacles of debauchery and
baseness, and those Schools that trains up Youth, as
well as Age, to ruine), in this Province there are
none; neither hath Youth his swing or range in such
a profuse and unbridled liberty as in other Countries;
for from an antient Custom at the primitive seating
of the place, the Son works as well as the Servant (an
excellent cure for untam'd Youth), so that before they
eat their bread, they are commonly taught how to
earn it; which makes them by that time Age speaks
them capable of receiving that which their Parents
indulgency is ready to give them, and which partly
is by their own laborious industry purchased, they
manage it with such a serious, grave and watching
care, as if they had been Masters of Families, trained
up in that domestick and governing power from their
Cradles. These Christian Natives of the Land, espe-

7

cially those of the Masculine Sex, are generally conveniently confident, reservedly subtile, quick in
apprehending, but slow in resolving; and where they
spy profit sailing towards them with the wings of a
prosperous gale, there they become much familiar.
The Women differ something in this point, though
not much : They are extreme bashful at the first
view, but after a continuance of time hath brought
them acquainted, there they become discreetly familiar, and are much more talkative then men. All
Complemental Courtships, drest up in critical Rarities,
are meer strangers to them, plain wit comes nearest
their Genius; so that he that intends to Court a
Mary-Land Girle, must have something more than
the Tautologies of a long-winded speech to carry on
his design, or else he may (for ought I know) fall
under the contempt of her frown, and his own windy
Oration.   (See note No. 30).

One great part of the Inhabitants of this Province
are desiredly Zealous, great pretenders to Holiness;
and where any thing appears that carries on the
Frontispiece of its Effigies the stamp of Religion,
though fundamentally never so imperfect, they are
suddenly taken with it, and out of an eager desire to
any thing that's new, not weighing the sure matter in
the Ballance of Reason, are very apt to be catcht.
(See note No. 31).   *Quakerism* is the only Opinion
that bears the Bell away (see note No. 32): The
Anabaptists (see note No. 33) have little to say here,

as well as in other places, since the Ghost of *John* of *Leyden* haunts their Conventicles. The *Adamite*, *Ranter*, and *Fift-Monarchy men*, *Mary-Land* cannot, nay will not digest within her liberal stomach such corroding morsels : So that this Province is an utter Enemy to blasphemous and zealous Imprecations, drain'd from the Lymbeck of hellish and damnable Spirits, as well as profuse prophaness, that issues from the prodigality of none but cract-brain Sots.

> ' *Tis said the Gods lower down that Chain above,*
> *That tyes both Prince and Subject up in Love ;*
> *And if this Fiction of the Gods be true,*
> *Few,* Mary-Land, *in this can boast but you :*
> *Live ever blest, and let those Clouds that do*
> *Eclipse most States, be always Lights to you ;*
> *And dwelling so, you may for ever be*
> *The only Emblem of Tranquility.*

CHAP. III.

The necessariness of Servitude proved, with the common usage of Servants in Mary-Land, *together with their Priviledges.*

A S there can be no Monarchy without the Supremacy of a King and Crown, nor no King without Subjects, nor any Parents without it be by the fruitful off-spring of Children; neither can there be any Masters, unless it be by the inferior Servitude of those that dwell under them, by a commanding enjoynment: And since it is ordained from the original and superabounding wisdom of all things, That there should be Degrees and Diversities amongst the Sons of men, in acknowledging of a Superiority from Inferiors to Superiors; the Servant with a reverent and befitting Obedience is as liable to this duty in a measurable performance to him whom he serves, as the loyalest of Subjects to his Prince. Then since it is a common and ordained Fate, that there must be Servants as well as Masters, and that good Servitudes are those Colledges of Sobriety that checks in the giddy and wild-headed youth from his profuse and uneven course of life, by a limited constrainment, as well as it otherwise agrees with the moderate and discreet Servant: Why should there be such an exclusive

Obstacle in the minds and unreasonable dispositions of many people, against the limited time of convenient and necessary Servitude, when it is a thing so requisite, that the best of Kingdoms would be unhing'd from their quiet and well setled Government without it. Which levelling doctrine we here of *England* in this latter age (whose womb was truss'd out with nothing but confused Rebellion) have too much experienced, and was daily rung into the ears of the tumultuous Vulgar by the Bell-weather Sectaries of the Times: But (blessed be God) those Clouds are blown over, and the Government of the Kingdom coucht under a more stable form.

There is no truer Emblem of Confusion either in Monarchy or Domestick Governments, then when either the Subject, or the Servant, strives for the upper hand of his Prince, or Master, and to be equal with him, from whom he receives his present subsistance: Why then, if Servitude be so necessary that no place can be governed in order, nor people live without it, this may serve to tell those which prick up their ears and bray against it, That they are none but Asses, and deserve the Bridle of a strict commanding power to reine them in: For I'me certainly confident, that there are several Thousands in most Kingdoms of Christendom, that could not at all live and subsist, unless they had served some prefixed time, to learn either some Trade, Art, or Science, and by either of them to extract their present livelihood.

Then methinks this may stop the mouths of those that will undiscreetly compassionate them that dwell under necessary Servitudes; for let but Parents of an indifferent capacity in Estates, when their Childrens age by computation speak them seventeen or eighteen years old, turn them loose to the wide world, without a seven years working Apprenticeship (being just brought up to the bare formality of a little reading and writing) and you shall immediately see how weak and shiftless they'le be towards the maintaining and supporting of themselves; and (without either stealing or begging) their bodies like a Sentinel must continually wait to see when their Souls will be frighted away by the pale Ghost of a starving want.

Then let such, where Providence hath ordained to live as Servants, either in *England* or beyond Sea, endure the prefixed yoak of their limited time with patience, and then in a small computation of years, by an industrious endeavour, they may become Masters and Mistresses of Families themselves. And let this be spoke to the deserved praise of *Mary-Land*, That the four years I served there were not to me so slavish, as a two years Servitude of a Handicraft Apprenticeship was here in *London; Volenti enim nil difficile:* Not that I write this to seduce or delude any, or to draw them from their native soyle, but out of a love to my Countrymen, whom in the general I wish well to, and that the lowest of them may live in such a capacity of Estate, as that the bare interest of their Livelihoods might not altogether depend upon persons of the greatest extendments.

Now those whose abilities here in *England* are capable of maintaining themselves in any reasonable and handsom manner, they had best so to remain, lest the roughness of the Ocean, together with the staring visages of the wilde Animals, which they may see after their arrival into the Country, may alter the natural dispositions of their bodies, that the stay'd and solid part that kept its motion by Doctor *Trigs* purgationary operation, may run beyond the byas of the wheel in a violent and laxative confusion.

Now contrarywise, they who are low, and make bare shifts to buoy themselves up above the shabby center of beggarly and incident casualties, I heartily could wish the removal of some of them into *Mary-Land*, which would make much better for them that stay'd behind, as well as it would advantage those that went.

They whose abilities cannot extend to purchase their own transportation into *Mary-Land* (and surely he that cannot command so small a sum for so great a matter, his life must needs be mighty low and dejected), I say they may for the debarment of a four years sordid liberty, go over into this Province and there live plentiously well. And what's a four years Servitude to advantage a man all the remainder of his dayes, making his predecessors happy in his sufficient abilities, which he attained to partly by the restrainment of so small a time?

Now those that commit themselves into the care of the Merchant to carry them over, they need not trouble themselves with any inquisitive search touching their Voyage; for there is such an honest care and provision made for them all the time they remain aboard the Ship, and are sailing over, that they want for nothing that is necessary and convenient.

The Merchant commonly before they go aboard the Ship, or set themselves in any forwardness for their Voyage, has Conditions of Agreements drawn between him and those that by a voluntary consent become his Servants, to serve him, his Heirs or Assigns, according as they in their primitive acquaintance have made their bargain (see note No. 34), some two, some three, some four years; and whatever the Master or Servant tyes himself up to here in *England* by Condition, the Laws of the Province will force a performance of when they come there: Yet here is this Priviledge in it when they arrive, If they dwell not with the Merchant they made their first agreement withall, they may choose whom they will serve their prefixed time with; and after their curiosity has pitcht on one whom they think fit for their turn, and that they may live well withall, the Merchant makes an Assignment of the Indenture over to him whom they of their free will have chosen to be their Master, in the same nature as we here in *England* (and no

otherwise) turn over Covenant Servants or Apprentices from one Master to another.   Then let those
whose chaps are always breathing forth those filthy
dregs of abusive exclamations, which are Lymbeckt
from their sottish and preposterous brains, against
this Country of *Mary-Land*, saying, That those which
are transported over thither, are sold in open Market
for Slaves, and draw in Carts like Horses; which is
so damnable an untruth, that if they should search to
the very Center of Hell, and enquire for a Lye of the
most antient and damned stamp, I confidently believe
they could not find one to parallel this: For know,
That the Servants here in *Mary-Land* of all Colonies,
distant or remote Plantations, have the least cause to
complain, either for strictness of Servitude, want of
Provisions, or need of Apparel: Five dayes and a half
in the Summer weeks is the alotted time that they
work in; and for two months, when the Sun predomi-
nates in the highest pitch of his heat, they claim an
antient and customary Priviledge, to repose themselves
three hours in the day within the house, and this is
undeniably granted to them that work in the Fields.

In the Winter time, which lasteth three months
(viz.), *December, January*, and *February*, they do little
or no work or imployment, save cutting of wood to
make good fires to sit by, unless their Ingenuity will
prompt them to hunt the Deer, or Bear, or recreate
themselves in Fowling, to slaughter the Swans, Geese,
and Turkeys (which this Country affords in a most

8

plentiful manner) : For every Servant has a Gun,
Powder and Shot allowed him, to sport him withall
on all Holidayes and leasurable times, if he be capable
of using it, or be willing to learn.

Now those Servants which come over into this
Province, being Artificers, they never (during their
Servitude) work in the Fields, or do any other imployment save that which their Handicraft and Mechanick
endeavours are capable of putting them upon, and are
esteem'd as well by their Masters, as those that imploy
them, above measure. He that's a Tradesman here
in *Mary-Land* (though a Servant), lives as well as
most common Handicrafts do in *London*, though they
may want something of that Liberty which Freemen
have, to go and come at their pleasure ; yet if it were
rightly understood and considered, what most of the
Liberties of the several poor Tradesmen are taken up
about, and what a care and trouble attends that thing
they call Liberty, which according to the common
translation is but Idleness, and (if weighed in the
Ballance of a just Reason) will be found to be much
heavier and cloggy then the four years restrainment
of a *Mary-Land* Servitude. He that lives in the
nature of a Servant in this Province, must serve but
four years by the Custom of the Country ; and when
the expiration of his time speaks him a Freeman,
there's a Law in the Province, that enjoyns his Master
whom he hath served to give him Fifty Acres of Land,
Corn to serve him a whole year, three Suits of Apparel,

with things necessary to them, and Tools to work withall; so that they are no sooner free, but they are ready to set up for themselves, and when once entred, they live passingly well.   (See note No. 35).

The Women that go over into this Province as Servants, have the best luck here as in any place of the world besides; for they are no sooner on shoar, but they are courted into a Copulative Matrimony, which some of them (for aught I know) had they not come to such a Market with their Virginity, might have kept it by them untill it had been mouldy, unless they had let it out by a yearly rent to some of the Inhabitants of *Lewknors-Lane* (see note No. 36), or made a Deed of Gift of it to Mother *Coney*, having only a poor stipend out of it, untill the Gallows or Hospital called them away.   Men have not altogether so good luck as Women in this kind, or natural preferment, without they be good Rhetoricians, and well vers'd in the Art of perswasion, then (probably) they may ryvet themselves in the time of their Servitude into the private and reserved favour of their Mistress, if Age speak their Master deficient.

In short, touching the Servants of this Province, they live well in the time of their Service, and by their restrainment in that time, they are made capable of living much better when they come to be free; which in several other parts of the world I have observed, That after some servants have brought their indented and limited time to a just and legal period

by Servitude, they have been much more incapable of
supporting themselves from sinking into the Gulf of a
slavish, poor, fettered, and intangled life, then all the
fastness of their prefixed time did involve them in
before.

Now the main and principal Reason of those incident casualties, that wait continually upon the resi-
dences of most poor Artificers, is (I gather) from the
multiciplicity or innumerableness of those several
Companies of Tradesmen, that dwell so closely and
stiflingly together in one and the same place, that
like the chafing Gum in Watered-Tabby, they eat into
the folds of one anothers Estates. And this might
easily be remedied, would but some of them remove
and disperse distantly where want and necessity calls
for them; their dwellings (I am confident) would be
much larger, and their conditions much better, as well
in reference to their Estates, as to the satisfactoriness
of their minds, having a continual imployment, and
from that imployment a continual benefit, without
either begging, seducing, or flattering for it, encroach-
ing that one month from one of the same profession,
that they are heaved out themselves the next. For
I have observed on the other side of *Mary-Land*, that
the whole course of most Mechanical endeavours, is
to catch, snatch, and undervalue one another, to get
a little work, or a Customer; which when they have
attained by their lowbuilt and sneaking circumvent-
ings, it stands upon so flashy, mutable, and transitory

a foundation, that the best of his hopes is commonly extinguisht before the poor undervalued Tradesman is warm in the enjoyment of his Customer.

Then did not a cloud of low and base Cowardize eclipse the Spirits of these men, these things might easily be diverted; but they had as live take a Bear by the tooth, as think of leaving their own Country, though they live among their own National people, and are governed by the same Laws they have here, yet all this wont do with them; and all the Reason they can render to the contrary is, There's a great Sea betwixt them and *Mary-Land*, and in that Sea there are Fishes, and not only Fishes but great Fishes, and then should a Ship meet with such an inconsiderable encounter as a Whale, one blow with his tayle, and then *Lord have Mercy upon us :* Yet meet with these men in their common Exchange, which is one story high in the bottom of a Celler, disputing over a Black-pot, it would be monstrously dreadful here to insert the particulars, one swearing that he was the first that scaled the Walls of *Dundee,* when the Bullets flew about their ears as thick as Hailstones usually fall from the Sky; which if it were but rightly examined, the most dangerous Engagement that ever he was in, was but at one of the flashy battels at *Finsbury* (see note No. 37), where commonly there's more Custard greedily devoured, than men prejudiced by the rigour of the War. Others of this Company relating their several dreadful exploits,

and when they are just entring into the particulars,
let but one step in and interrupt their discourse, by
telling them of a Sea Voyage, and the violency of
storms that attends it, and that there are no back-
doors to run out at, which they call, *a handsom
Retreat and Charge again;* the apprehensive danger
of this is so powerful and penetrating on them, that a
damp sweat immediately involves their Microcosm,
so that *Margery* the old Matron of the Celler, is fain
to run for a half-peny-worth of *Angelica* to rub their
nostrils; and though the Port-hole of their bodies
has been stopt from a convenient Evacuation some
several months, theyl'e need no other Suppository to
open the Orifice of their Esculent faculties then this
Relation, as their Drawers or Breeches can more at
large demonstrate to the inquisitive search of the
curious.

Now I know that some will be apt to judge, that I
have written this last part out of derision to some of
my poor Mechanick Country-men: Truly I must
needs tell those to their face that think so of me, that
they prejudice me extremely, by censuring me as
guilty of any such crime: What I have written is
only to display the sordidness of their dispositions,
who rather than they will remove to another Country
to live plentiously well, and give their Neighbors
more Elbow-room and space to breath in, they will
croud and throng upon one another, with the pressure
of a beggarly and unnecessary weight.

That which I have to say more in this business, is a hearty and desirous wish, that the several poor Tradesmen here in *London* that I know, and have borne an occular testimony of their want, might live so free from care as I did when I dwelt in the bonds of a four years Servitude in *Mary-Land*.

Be just (Domestick Monarchs) unto them
That dwell as Household Subjects to each Realm;
Let not your Power make you be too severe,
Where there's small faults reign in your sharp Career:
So that the Worlds base yelping Crew
May'nt bark what I have wrote is writ untrue,
So use your Servants, if there come no more,
They may serve Eight, instead of serving Four.

CHAP. IV.

Upon Trafique, and what Merchandizing Commodities this Province affords, also how Tobacco is planted and made fit for Commerce.

TRafique, Commerce, and Trade, are those great wheeles that by their circular and continued motion, turn into most Kingdoms of the Earth the plenty of abundant Riches that they are commonly fed withall: For Trafique in his right description, is the very soul of a Kingdom; and should but Fate ordain a removal of it for some years, from the richest and most populous Monarchy that dwells in the most fertile clyme of the whole Universe, he would soon find by a woful experiment, the miss and loss of so reviving a supporter. And I am certainly confident, that *England* would as soon feel her feebleness by withdrawment of so great an upholder; as well in reference to the internal and healthful preservative of her Inhabitants, for want of those Medicinal Drugs that are landed upon her Coast every year, as the external profits, Glory and beneficial Graces that accrue by her.

Paracelsus might knock down his Forge, if Trafique and Commerce should once cease, and grynde the hilt of his Sword into Powder, and take some of the Infusion to make him so valorous, that he might cut his own Throat in the honor of *Mercury : Galen* might then burn his Herbal, and like *Joseph of Arimathea,* build him a Tomb in his Garden, and so rest from his labours : Our Physical Collegians of *London* would have no cause then to thunder Fire-balls at *Nich. Culpeppers* Dispensatory (see note No. 38). All Herbs, Roots, and Medicines would bear their original christening, that the ignorant might understand them : *Album grecum* would not be *Album grecum* (see note No. 39) then, but a Dogs turd would be a Dogs turd in plain terms, in spight of their teeth.

If Trade should once cease, the Custom-house would soon miss her hundreds and thousands Hogs-heads of Tobacco (see note No. 40), that use to be throng in her every year, as well as the Grocers would in their Ware-houses and Boxes, the Gentry and Commonalty in their Pipes, the Physician in his Drugs and Medicinal Compositions; The (leering) Waiters for want of imployment, might (like so many *Diogenes*) intomb themselves in their empty Casks, and rouling themselves off the Key into the *Thames,* there wander up and down from tide to tide in contemplation of *Aristotles* unresolved curiosity, until the rottenness of their circular habitation give them a *Quietus est,* and fairly surrender them up into the custody of those who both for profession, disposition and nature, lay as near claim to them, as if they both tumbled in one belly, and for name they jump alike, being according to the original translation both *Sharkes.*

9

Silks and Cambricks, and Lawns to make sleeves, would be as soon miss'd at Court, as Gold and Silver would be in the Mint and Pockets: The Low-Country Soldier would be at a cold stand for Outlandish Furrs to make him Muffs, to keep his ten similitudes warm in the Winter, as well as the Furrier for want of Skins to uphold his Trade.

Should Commerce once cease, there is no Country in the habitable world but would undoubtedly miss that flourishing, splendid and rich gallantry of Equipage, that Trafique maintained and drest her up in, before she received that fatal Eclipse: *England, France, Germany* and *Spain,* together with all the Kingdoms ——

But stop (good Muse) lest I should, like the Parson of *Pancras* (see note No. 41), run so far from my Text in half an hour, that a two hours trot back again would hardly fetch it up: I had best while I am alive in my Doctrine, to think again of *Mary-Land,* lest the business of other Countries take up so much room in my brain, that I forget and bury her in oblivion.

The three main Commodities this Country affords for Trafique, are Tobacco, Furrs, and Flesh. Furrs and Skins, as Beavers, Otters, Musk-Rats, Rackoons, Wild-Cats, and Elke or Buffeloe (see note No. 42), with divers others, which were first made vendible by the *Indians* of the Country, and sold to the Inhabitant, and by them to the Merchant, and so transported into *England* and other places where it becomes most commodious.

Tobacco is the only solid Staple Commodity of this Province: The use of it was first found out by the *Indians* many Ages agoe, and transferr'd into Christendom by that great Discoverer of *America Columbus*. It's generally made by all the Inhabitants of this Province, and between the months of *March* and *April* they sow the seed (which is much smaller then Mustard-seed) in small beds and patches digg'd up and made so by art, and about *May* the Plants commonly appear green in those beds: In *June* they are transplanted from their beds, and set in little hillocks in distant rowes, dug up for the same purpose; some twice or thrice they are weeded, and succoured from their illegitimate Leaves that would be peeping out from the body of the Stalk. They top the several Plants as they find occasion in their predominating rankness: About the middle of *September* they cut the Tobacco down, and carry it into houses, (made for that purpose) to bring it to its purity: And after it has attained, by a convenient attendance upon time, to its perfection, it is then tyed up in bundles, and packt into Hogs-heads, and then laid by for the Trade.

Between *November* and *January* there arrives in this Province Shipping to the number of twenty sail and upwards (see note No. 43), all Merchant-men loaden with Commodities to Trafique and dispose of,

trucking with the Planter for Silks, Hollands, Serges,
and Broad-clothes, with other necessary Goods, priz'd
at such and such rates as shall be judg'd on is fair
and legal, for Tobacco at so much the pound, and
advantage on both sides considered; the Planter for
his work, and the Merchant for adventuring himself
and his Commodity into so far a Country: Thus is the
Trade on both sides drove on with a fair and honest
Decorum.

The Inhabitants of this Province are seldom or
never put to the affrightment of being robb'd of their
money, nor to dirty their Fingers by telling of vast
sums: They have more bags to carry Corn, then
Coyn; and though they want, but why should I call
that a want which is only a necessary miss? the very
effects of the dirt of this Province affords as great a
profit to the general Inhabitant, as the Gold of *Peru*
doth to the straight-breecht Commonalty of the
Spaniard.

Our Shops and Exchanges of *Mary-Land*, are the
Merchants Store-houses, where with few words and
protestations Goods are bought and delivered; not
like those Shop-keepers Boys in *London*, that continually cry, *What do ye lack Sir? What d'ye buy?*
yelping with so wide a mouth, as if some Apothecary
had hired their mouths to stand open to catch Gnats
and Vagabond Flyes in.

Tobacco is the currant Coyn of *Mary-Land*, and
will sooner purchase Commodities from the Merchant,

then money. I must confess the *New-England* men
that trade into this Province, had rather have fat
Pork for their Goods, than Tobacco or Furrs (see note
No. 44), which I conceive is, because their bodies
being fast bound up with the cords of restringent
Zeal, they are fain to make use of the lineaments
of this *Non-Canaanite* creature physically to loosen
them; for a bit of a pound upon a two-peny Rye loaf,
according to the original Receipt, will bring the cos-
tiv'st red-ear'd Zealot in some three hours time to a
fine stool, if methodically observed.

Medera-Wines, Sugars, Salt, Wickar-Chairs, and
Tin Candlesticks, is the most of the Commodities they
bring in : They arrive in *Mary-Land* about *September*,
being most of them Ketches and Barkes, and such
small Vessels, and those dispersing themselves into
several small Creeks of this Province, to sell and dispose of their Commodities, where they know the
Market is most fit for their small Adventures.

Barbadoes (see note No. 45), together with the
several adjacent Islands, has much Provision yearly
from this Province : And though these Sun-burnt
Phaetons think to outvye *Mary-Land* in their Silks
and Puffs, daily speaking against her whom their
necessities makes them beholding to, and like so
many *Don Diegos* that becackt *Pauls*, cock their Felts
and look big upon't; yet if a man could go down into
their infernals, and see how it fares with them there,
I believe he would hardly find any other Spirit to

buoy them up, then the ill-visaged Ghost of want, that continually wanders from gut to gut to feed upon the undigested rynes of Potatoes.

Trafique is Earth's great Atlas, that supports
The pay of Armies, and the height of Courts,
And makes Mechanicks live, that else would die
Meer starving Martyrs to their penury :
None but the Merchant of this thing can boast,
He, like the Bee, comes loaden from each Coast,
And to all Kingdoms, as within a Hive,
Stows up those Riches that doth make them thrive :
Be thrifty, Mary-Land, *keep what thou hast in store,*
And each years Trafique to thy self get more.

A Relation of the Customs, Manners, Absurdities, and
Religion of the Susquehanock (see note No. 46)
Indians in and near Mary-Land.

A S the diversities of Languages (since Babels confusion) has made the distinction between people
and people, in this Christendompart of the world; so
are they distinguished Nation from Nation, by the
diversities and confusion of their Speech and Languages (see note No. 47) here in *America*: And as
every Nation differs in their Laws, Manners and Customs, in *Europe*, *Asia* and *Africa*, so do they the very
same here; That it would be a most intricate and
laborious trouble, to run (with a description) through
the several Nations of *Indians* here in *America*, considering the innumerableness and diversities of them
that dwell on this vast and unmeasured Continent:
But rather then I'le be altogether silent, I shall do
like the Painter in the Comedy, who being to limne
out the Pourtraiture of the Furies, as they severally
appeared, set himself behind a Pillar, and between
fright and amazement, drew them by guess. Those
Indians that I have convers'd withall here in this
Province of *Mary-Land*, and have had any occular
experimental view of either of their Customs, Manners, Religions, and Absurdities, are called by the

name of *Susquehanocks,* being a people lookt upon by
the Christian Inhabitants, as the most Noble and
Heroick Nation of *Indians* that dwell upon the confines of *America ;* also are so allowed and lookt upon
by the rest of the *Indians,* by a submissive and tribu-
tary acknowledgement; being a people cast into the
mould of a most large and Warlike deportment, the
men being for the most part seven foot high in lati-
tude, and in magnitude and bulk suitable to so high
a pitch ; their voyce large and hollow, as ascending
out of a Cave, their gate and behavior strait, stately
and majestick, treading on the Earth with as much
pride, contempt, and disdain to so sordid a Center,
as can be imagined from a creature derived from the
same mould and Earth.

Their bodies are cloth'd with no other Armour to
defend them from the nipping frosts of a benumbing
Winter, or the penetrating and scorching influence of
the Sun in a hot Summer, then what Nature gave
them when they parted with the dark receptacle of
their mothers womb.   They go Men, Women and
Children, all naked, only where shame leads them by
a natural instinct to be reservedly modest, there they
become cover'd.   The formality of *Jezabels* artificial
Glory is much courted and followed by these *Indians,*
only in matter of colours (I conceive) they differ.

The *Indians* paint upon their faces one stroke of
red, another of green, another of white, and another
of black, so that when they have accomplished the

Equipage of their Countenance in this trim, they are
the only Hieroglyphicks and Representatives of the
Furies. Their skins are naturally white, but altered
from their originals by the several dyings of Roots
and Barks, that they prepare and make useful to
metamorphize their hydes into a dark Cinamon brown.
The hair of their head is black, long and harsh, but
where Nature hath appointed the situation of it any
where else, they divert it (by an antient custom) from
its growth, by pulling it up hair by hair by the root
in its primitive appearance. Several of them wear
divers impressions on their breasts and armes, as the
picture of the Devil, Bears, Tigers, and Panthers,
which are imprinted on their several lineaments with
much difficulty and pain, with an irrevocable determi-
nation of its abiding there: And this they count a
badge of Heroick Valour, and the only Ornament due
to their *Heroes.* (See note No. 48).

These *Susquehanock Indians* are for the most part
great Warriours, and seldom sleep one Summer in the
quiet armes of a peaceable Rest, but keep (by their
present Power, as well as by their former Conquest)
the several Nations of *Indians* round about them, in a
forceable obedience and subjection.

Their Government is wrapt up in so various and
intricate a Laborynth, that the speculativ'st Artist in
the whole World, with his artificial and natural
Opticks, cannot see into the rule or sway of these
Indians, to distinguish what name of Government to

10

call them by; though *Purchas* (see note No. 49) in
his *Peregrination* between *London* and *Essex,* (which
he calls the whole World) will undertake (forsooth)
to make a Monarchy of them, but if he had said
Anarchy, his word would have pass'd with a better
belief.   All that ever I could observe in them as to
this matter is, that he that is most cruelly Valorous,
is accounted the most Noble: Here is very seldom
any creeping from a Country Farm, into a Courtly
Gallantry, by a sum of money; nor feeing the Heralds
to put Daggers and Pistols into their Armes, to make
the ignorant believe that they are lineally descended
from the house of the Wars and Conquests; he that
fights best carries it here.

When they determine to go upon some Design that
will and doth require a Consideration, some six of
them get into a corner, and sit in Juncto; and if
thought fit, their business is made popular, and immediately put into action; if not, they make a full stop
to it, and are silently reserv'd.

The Warlike Equipage they put themselves in
when they prepare for *Belona's* March, is with their
faces, armes, and breasts confusedly painted, their
hair greased with Bears oyl, and stuck thick with
Swans Feathers, with a wreath or Diadem of black
and white Beads upon their heads, a small Hatchet,
instead of a Cymetre, stuck in their girts behind them,
and either with Guns, or Bows and Arrows.   In this
posture and dress they march out from their Fort, or

dwelling, to the number of Forty in a Troop, singing (or rather howling out) the Decades or Warlike exploits of their Ancestors, ranging the wide Woods untill their fury has met with an Enemy worthy of their Revenge. What Prisoners fall into their hands by the destiny of War, they treat them very civilly while they remain with them abroad, but when they once return homewards, they then begin to dress them in the habit for death, putting on their heads and armes wreaths of Beads, greazing their hair with fat, some going before, and the rest behind, at equal distance from their Prisoners, bellowing in a strange and confused manner, which is a true presage and forerunner of destruction to their then conquered Enemy. (See note No. 50).

In this manner of march they continue till they have brought them to their Berken City (see note No. 51), where they deliver them up to those that in cruelty will execute them, without either the legal Judgement of a Council of War, or the benefit of their Clergy at the Common Law. The common and usual deaths they put their Prisoners to, is to bind them to stakes, making a fire some distance from them; then one or other of them, whose Genius delights in the art of Paganish dissection, with a sharp knife or flint cuts the Cutis or outermost skin of the brow so deep, untill their nails, or rather Talons, can fasten themselves firm and secure in, then (with a most rigid jerk) disrobeth the head of skin and hair at one pull, leaving the skull almost as bare as those Monumental Skelitons at Chyrurgions-Hall; but for fear they should get cold by leaving so warm and customary a Cap off, they immediately apply to the skull a Cataplasm of hot Embers to keep their Pericanium warm. While they are thus acting this cruelty on their heads, several others are preparing pieces of Iron, and barrels of old Guns, which they make red hot, to sear each part and lineament of their bodies, which they perform and act in a most cruel and barbarous manner: And while they are thus in the midst of their torments and execrable usage, some tearing their skin and hair of their head off by violence, others searing their bodies with hot irons, some are cutting their flesh off, and eating it before their eyes raw while they are alive; yet all this and much more never makes them lower the Top-gallant sail of their Heroick courage, to beg with a submissive Repentance any indulgent favour from their persecuting Enemies; but with an undaunted contempt to their cruelty, eye it with so slight and mean a respect, as if it were below them to value what they did, they courageously (while breath doth libertize them) sing the summary of their Warlike Atchievements.

Now after this cruelty has brought their tormented lives to a period, they immediately fall to butchering of them into parts, distributing the several pieces amongst the Sons of War, to intomb the ruines of their deceased Conquest in no other Sepulchre then their unsanctified maws; which they with more appetite and desire do eat and digest, then if the best of foods should court their stomachs to participate of the most restorative Banquet. Yet though they now and then feed upon the Carkesses of their Enemies, this is not a common dyet, but only a particular dish for the better sort (see note No. 52); for there is not a Beast that runs in the Woods of *America*, but if they can by any means come at him, without any scruple of Conscience they'le fall too (without saying Grace) with a devouring greediness.

As for their Religion, together with their Rites and Ceremonies, they are so absurd and ridiculous, that its almost a sin to name them. They own no other Deity than the Devil, (solid or profound) but with a kind of a wilde imaginary conjecture, they suppose from their groundless conceits, that the World had a Maker, but where he is that made it, or whether he be living to this day, they know not. The Devil, as I said before, is all the God they own or worship; and that more out of a slavish fear then any real Reverence to his Infernal or Diabolical greatness, he forcing them to their Obedience by his rough and rigid dealing with them, often appearing visibly among them to their terrour, bastinadoing them (with cruel menaces) even unto death, and burning their Fields of Corn and houses, that the relation thereof makes them tremble themselves when they tell it.

Once in four years they Sacrifice a Childe to him (see note No. 53), in an acknowledgement of their firm obedience to all his Devillish powers, and Hellish commands. The Priests to whom they apply themselves in matters of importance and greatest distress, are like those that attended upon the Oracle at *Delphos*, who by their Magic-spells could command a *pro* or *con* from the Devil when they pleas'd. These *Indians* oft-times raise great Tempests when they have any weighty matter or design in hand, and by blustering storms inquire of their Infernal God (the Devil) *How matters shall go with them either in publick or private.* (See note No. 54). .

When any among them depart this life, they give him no other intombment, then to set him upright upon his breech in a hole dug in the Earth some five foot long, and three foot deep, covered over with the Bark of Trees Arch-wise, with his face Du-West, only leaving a hole half a foot square open. They dress him in the same Equipage and Gallantry that he used to be trim'd in when he was alive, and so bury him (if a Soldier) with his Bows, Arrows, and Target, together with all the rest of his implements and weapons of War, with a Kettle of Broth, and Corn standing before him, lest he should meet with bad quarters in his way. (See note No. 55). His Kinred and Relations follow him to the Grave, sheath'd in Bear skins for close mourning, with the tayl droyling on the ground, in imitation of our *English* Solemners,

that think there's nothing like a tayl a Degree in
length, to follow the dead Corpse to the Grave with.
Here if that snuffling Prolocutor, that waits upon the
dead Monuments of the Tombs at *Westminster*, with
his white Rod were there, he might walk from Tomb
to Tomb with his, *Here lies the Duke of* Ferrara *and
his Dutchess*, and never find any decaying vacation,
unless it were in the moldering Consumption of his
own Lungs. They bury all within the wall or
Pallisado'd impalement of their City, or *Connadago*
(see note No. 56) as they call it. Their houses are
low and long, built with the Bark of Trees Arch-wise,
standing thick and confusedly together. They are
situated a hundred and odd miles distant from the
Christian Plantations of *Mary-Land*, at the head of a
River that runs into the Bay of *Chœsapike*, called by
their own name *The Susquehanock River*, where they
remain and inhabit most part of the Summer time,
and seldom remove far from it, unless it be to subdue
any Forreign Rebellion.

About *November* the best Hunters draw off to
several remote places of the Woods, where they know
the Deer, Bear, and Elke useth; there they build them
several Cottages, which they call their Winter-quarter,
where they remain for the space of three months, untill
they have killed up a sufficiency of Provisions to supply their Families with in the Summer.

The Women are the Butchers, Cooks, and Tillers
of the ground, the Men think it below the honour of

a Masculine, to stoop to any thing but that which
their Gun, or Bow and Arrows can command. The
Men kill the several Beasts which they meet withall
in the Woods, and the Women are the Pack horses to
fetch it in upon their backs, fleying and dressing the
hydes, (as well as the flesh for provision) to make
them fit for Trading, and which are brought down to
the *English* at several seasons in the year, to truck
and dispose of them for course Blankets, Guns, Powder and lead, Beads, small Looking-glasses, Knives,
and Razors.   (See note No. 57).

I never observed all the while I was amongst these
naked *Indians*, that ever the Women wore the
Breeches, or dared either in look or action predominate over the Men.   They are very constant to their
Wives; and let this be spoken to their Heathenish
praise, that did they not alter their bodies by their
dyings, paintings, and cutting themselves, marring
those Excellencies that Nature bestowed upon them
in their original conceptions and birth, there would
be as amiable beauties amongst them, as any *Alex-
andria* could afford, when *Mark Anthony* and *Cleo-
patra* dwelt there together.   Their Marriages are
short and authentique; for after 'tis resolv'd upon by
both parties, the Woman sends her intended Husband
a Kettle of boyl'd Venison, or Bear; and he returns
in lieu thereof Beaver or Otters Skins, and so their
Nuptial Rites are concluded without other Ceremony.
(See note No. 58).

Before I bring my Heathenish Story to a period, I have one thing worthy your observation : For as our Grammar Rules have it, *Non decet quenquam me ire currentem aut mandantem :* It doth not become any man to piss running or eating. These Pagan men naturally observe the same Rule; for they are so far from running, that like a Hare, they squat to the ground as low as they can, while the Women stand bolt upright with their armes a Kimbo, performing the same action, in so confident and obscene a posture (see note No. 59), as if they had taken their Degrees of Entrance at *Venice,* and commenced Bawds of Art at *Legorne.*

A Collection of some Letters that were written by
the same Author, most of them in the
time of his Servitude.

To my much Honored Friend Mr. T. B.

Sir,

I Have lived with sorrow to see the Anointed of the
Lord tore from his Throne by the hands of Pari-
cides, and in contempt haled, in the view of God,
Angels and Men, upon a public Theatre, and there
murthered. I have seen the sacred Temple of the
Almighty, in scorn by Schismatics made the Receptacle of Theeves and Robbers; and those Religious
Prayers, that in devotion Evening and Morning were
offered up as a Sacrifice to our God, rent by Sacri-
legious hands, and made no other use of, then sold to
Brothel-houses to light Tobacco with.

Who then can stay, or will, to see things of so great
weight steer'd by such barbarous Hounds as these:
First, were there an *Egypt* to go down to, I would
involve my Liberty to them, upon condition ne'er
more to see my Country. What? live in silence
under the sway of such base actions, is to give consent; and though the lowness of my present Estate
and Condition, with the hazard I put my future dayes
upon, might plead a just excuse for me to stay at
home; but Heavens forbid: I'le rather serve in

Chains, and draw the Plough with Animals, till death shall stop and say, *It is enough.* Sir, if you stay behind, I wish you well: I am bound for *Mary-Land*, this day I have made some entrance into my intended voyage, and when I have done more, you shall know of it. I have here inclosed what you of me desired, but truly trouble, discontent and business, have so amazed my senses, that what to write, or where to write, I conceive my self almost as uncapable as he that never did write. What you'le find will be *Ex tempore*, without the use of premeditation; and though there may want something of a flourishing stile to dress them forth, yet I'm certain there wants nothing of truth, will, and desire.

Heavens bright Lamp, shine forth some of thy Light,
But just so long to paint this dismal Night;
Then draw thy beams, and hide thy glorious face,
From the dark sable actions of this place;
Leaving these lustful Sodomites groping still,
To satisfie each dark unsatiate will,
Untill at length the crimes that they commit,
May sink them down to Hells Infernal pit.
Base and degenerate Earth, how dost thou lye,
That all that pass hiss, at thy Treachery?
Thou which couldst boast once of thy King and Crown,
By base Mechanicks now art tumbled down,
Brewers *and* Coblers, *that have scarce an Eye,*
Walk hand in hand in thy Supremacy;
And all those Courts where Majesty did Throne,
Are now the Seats for Oliver and Ioan:

Persons of Honour, which did before inherit
Their glorious Titles from deserved merit,
Are all grown silent, and with wonder gaze,
To view such Slaves drest in their Courtly rayes;
To see a Drayman that knows nought but Yeast,
Set in a Throne like Babylons red Beast,
While heaps of Parasites do idolize
This red-nos'd Bell, with fawning Sacrifice.
What can we say? our King they've Murthered,
And those well born, are basely buried:
Nobles are slain, and Royalists in each street
Are scorn'd, and kick'd by most Men that they meet:
Religion's banisht, and Heresie survives,
And none but Conventicks in this Age thrives.
Oh could those Romans from their Ashes rise,
That liv'd in Nero's time: Oh how their cries
Would our perfidious Island shake, nay rend,
With clamorous screaks unto the Heaven send:
Oh how they'd blush to see our Crimson crimes,
And know the Subjects Authors of these times:
When as the Peasant he shall take his King,
And without cause shall fall a murthering him;
And when that's done, with Pride assume the Chair,
And Nimrod-like, himself to heaven rear;
Command the People, make the Land Obey
His baser will, and swear to what he'l say.
Sure, sure our God has not these evils sent
To please himself, but for mans punishment:
And when he shall from our dark sable Skies
Withdraw these Clouds, and let our Sun arise,
Our dayes will surely then in Glory shine,
Both in our Temporal, and our State divine:

May this come quickly, though I may never see
This glorious day, yet I would sympathie,
And feel a joy run through each vain of blood,
Though Vassalled on t'other side the Floud.
Heavens protect his Sacred Majesty,
From secret Plots, & treacherous Villany.
And that those Slaves that now predominate,
Hang'd and destroy'd may be their best of Fate;
And though Great Charles *be distant from his own,*
Heaven I hope will seat him on his Throne.

Vale.

Yours what I may,

G. A.

From the Chimney Corner upon a
    low cricket, where I writ this in
    the noise of some six Women,
Aug. 19.   *Anno*

To my Honored Father at his House.

SIR,

BEfore I dare bid Adieu to the old World, or
shake hands with my native Soyl for ever, I
have a Conscience inwards tells me, that I must offer
up the remains of that Obedience of mine, that lyes
close centered within the cave of my Soul, at the
Alter, of your paternal Love : And though this Sacrifice of mine may shew something low and thread-bare,
(at this time) yet know, That in the Zenith of all

actions, Obedience is that great wheel that moves the lesser in their circular motion.

I am now entring for some time to dwell under the Government of *Neptune*, a Monarchy that I was never manured to live under, nor to converse with in his dreadful Aspect, neither do I know how I shall bear with his rough demands; but that God has carried me through those many gusts a shoar, which I have met withall in the several voyages of my life, I hope will Pilot me safely to my desired Port, through the worst of Stormes I shall meet withall at Sea.

We have strange, and yet good news aboard, that he whose vast mind could not be contented with spacious Territories to stretch his insatiate desires on, is (by an Almighty power) banished from his usuped Throne to dwell among the dead. I no sooner heard of it, but my melancholly Muse forced me upon this ensuing Distich.

Poor vaunting Earth, gloss'd with uncertain Pride,
That liv'd in Pomp, yet worse than others dy'd :
Who shall blow forth a Trumpet to thy praise ?
Or call thy sable Actions shining Rayes ?
Such Lights as those blaze forth the vertued dead,
And make them live, though they are buried.
Thou'st gone, and to thy memory let be said,
There lies that Oliver which of old betray'd
His King and Master, and after did assume,
With swelling Pride, to govern in his room.
Here I'le rest satisfied, Scriptures expound to me,
Tophet was made for such Supremacy.

The death of this great Rebel (I hope) will prove
an *Omen* to presage destruction on the rest. The
World's in a heap of troubles and confusion, and
while they are in the midst of their changes and
amazes, the best way to give them the bag, is to go
out of the World and leave them. I am now bound
for *Mary-Land,* and I am told that's a New World,
but if it prove no better than this, I shall not get
much by my change; but before I'le revoke my
Resolution, I am resolv'd to put it to adventure, for I
think it can hardly be woise then this is: Thus com-
mitting you into the hands of that God that made
you, I rest

Your Obedient Son,

G. A.

From aboard a Ship at *Gravesend, Sept.* 7th, *Anno*

To my Brother.

I Leave you very near in the same condition as I
am in my self, only here lies the difference, you
were bound at Joyners Hall in *London* Apprentice-
wise, and I conditionally at Navigators Hall, that
now rides at an Anchor at *Gravesend ;* I hope you
will allow me to live in the largest Mayordom, by
reason I am the eldest: None but the main Continent
of *America* will serve me for a Corporation to inhabit

in now, though I am affraid for all that, that the
reins of my Liberty will be something shorter then
yours will be in *London:* But as to that, what Destiny has ordered I am resolved with an adventerous
Resolution to subscribe to, and with a contented
imbracement enjoy it. I would fain have seen you
once more in this Old World, before I go into the
New, I know you have a chain about your Leg, as
well as I have a clog about my Neck: If you can't
come, send a line or two, if not, wish me well at least:
I have one thing to charge home upon you, and I
hope you will take my counsel, That you have
alwayes an obedient Respect and Reverence to your
aged Parents, that while they live they may have
comfort of you, and when that God shall sound a
retreat to their lives, that there they may with their
gray hairs in joy go down to their Graves.

Thus concluding, wishing you a comfortable Servitude, a prosperous Life, and the assurance of a happy
departure in the immutable love of him that made
you, Vale.

Your Brother,

G. A.

From *Gravesend,* Sept. 7. *Anno*

To my much Honored Friend Mr. T. B. *at his House.*

I Am got ashoar with much ado, and it is very well it is as it is, for if I had stayed a little longer, I had certainly been a Creature of the Water, for I had hardly flesh enough to carry me to Land, not that I wanted for any thing that the Ship could afford me in reason: But oh the great bowls of Pease-porridge that appeared in sight every day about the hour of twelve, ingulfed the senses of my Appetite so, with the restringent quality of the Salt Beef, upon the internal Inhabitants of my belly, that a *Galenist* for some days after my arrival, with his Bag-pipes of Physical operations, could hardly make my Puddings dance in any methodical order.

But to set by these things that happened unto me at Sea, I am now upon Land, and there I'le keep my self if I can, and for four years I am pretty sure of my restraint; and had I known my yoak would have been so easie, (as I conceive it will) I would have been here long before now, rather then to have dwelt under the pressure of a Rebellious and Trayterous Government so long as I did. I dwell now by providence in the Province of *Mary-Land*, (under the quiet Government of the Lord *Baltemore*) which Country a bounds in a most glorious prosperity and plenty of all things. And though the Infancy of her situation might plead an excuse to those several imperfections, (if she were guilty of any of them) which by scandal-

ous and imaginary conjectures are falsly laid to her
charge, and which she values with so little notice or
perceivance of discontent, that she hardly alters her
visage with a frown, to let them know she is angry
with such a Rascality of people, that loves nothing
better then their own sottish and abusive acclama-
tions of baseness: To be short, the Country (so far
forth as I have seen into it) is incomparable.

Here is a sort of naked Inhabitants, or wilde
people, that have for many ages I believe lived here
in the Woods of *Mary-Land*, as well as in other parts
of the Continent, before e'er it was by the Christian
Discoverers found out; being a people strange to
behold, as well in their looks, which by confused
paintings makes them seem dreadful, as in their
sterne and heroick gate and deportments, the Men
are mighty tall and big limbed, the Women not altogether so large; they are most of them very well
featured, did not their wilde and ridiculous dresses
alter their original excellencies: The men are great
Warriours and Hunters, the Women ingenious and
laborious Housewives.

As to matter of their Worship, they own no other
Deity then the Devil, and him more out of a slavish
fear, then any real devotion, or willing acknowledgement to his Hellish power. They live in little small
Bark-Cottages, in the remote parts of the Woods,
killing and slaying the several Animals that they
meet withall to make provision of, dressing their

several Hydes and Skins to Trafique withall, when a
conveniency of Trade presents. I would go on further, but like Doctor *Case*, when he had not a word
more to speak for himself, *I am affraid my beloved I
have kept you too long.* Now he that made you save
you. *Amen.*

Yours to command,

G. A.

From *Mary-Land, Febr.* 6.   *Anno*

And not to forget *Tom Forge* I beseech you, tell
him that my Love's the same towards him still, and
as firm as it was about the overgrown Tryal, when
Judgements upon judgements, had not I stept in,
would have pursued him untill the day of Judgement, &c.

To my Father at his House.

SIR,

AFter my Obedience (at so great and vast a distance) has humbly saluted you and my good
Mother, with the cordialest of my prayers, wishes,
and desires to wait upon you, with the very best of
their effectual devotion, wishing from the very Center
of my Soul your flourishing and well-being here upon
Earth, and your glorious and everlasting happiness in
the World to Come.

These lines (my dear Parents) come from that Son which by an irregular Fate was removed from his Native home, and after a five months dangerous passage, was landed on the remote Continent of *America*, in the Province of *Mary-Land*, where now by providence I reside. To give you the particulars of the several accidents that happened in our voyage by Sea, it would swell a Journal of some sheets, and therefore too large and tedious for a Letter : I think it therefore necessary to bind up the relation in Octavo, and give it you in short.

We had a blowing and dangerous passage of it, and for some dayes after I arrived, I was an absolute *Copernicus*, it being one main point of my moral Creed, to believe the World had a pair of long legs, and walked with the burthen of the Creation upon her back. For to tell you the very truth of it, for some dayes upon Land, after so long and tossing a passage, I was so giddy that I could hardly tread an even step; so that all things both above and below (that was in view) appeared to me like the *Kentish Britains* to *William the Conqueror*, in a moving posture.

Those few number of weeks since my arrival, has given me but little experience to write any thing large of the Country; only thus much I can say, and that not from any imaginary conjectures, but from an occular observation, That this Country of *Mary-Land* abounds in a flourishing variety of delightful Woods, pleasant groves, lovely Springs, together with spacious Navigable Rivers and Creeks, it being a most helthful and pleasant situation, so far as my knowledge has yet had any view in it.

Herds of Deer are as numerous in this Province of *Mary-Land*, as Cuckolds can be in *London*, only their horns are not so well drest and tipt with silver as theirs are.

Here if the Devil had such a Vagary in his head as he had once among the *Gadareans*, he might drown a thousand head of Hogs and they'd ne're be miss'd, for the very Woods of this Province swarms with them.

The Christian Inhabitant of this Province, as to the general, lives wonderful well and contented: The Government of this Province is by the loyalness of the people, and loving demeanor of the Proprietor and Governor of the same, kept in a continued peace and unity.

The Servant of this Province, which are stigmatiz'd for Slaves by the clappermouth jaws of the vulgar in *England*, live more like Freemen then the most Mechanick Apprentices in *London*, wanting for nothing that is convenient and necessary, and according to their several capacities, are extraordinary well used and respected. So leaving things here as I found them, and lest I should commit · Sacriledge upon your more serious meditations, with the Tautologies of a long-winded Letter, I'le subscribe with a heavenly Ejaculation to the God of Mercy to preserve you now and for evermore, *Amen.*

Your Obedient Son,

G. A.

From *Mary-Land, Jan.* 17. *Anno*

To my much Honored Friend Mr. M. F.

SIR,

YOu writ to me when I was at *Gravesend,* (but I had no conveniency to send you an answer till now) enjoyning me, if possible, to give you a just Information by my diligent observance, what thing were best and most profitable to send into this Country for a commodious Trafique.

Sir, The enclosed will demonstrate unto you both particularly and at large, to the full satisfaction of your desire, it being an Invoyce drawn as exact to the business you imployed me upon, as my weak capacity could extend to.

Sir, If you send any Adventure to this Province, let me beg to give you this advice in it; That the Factor whom you imploy be a man of a Brain, otherwise the Planter will go near to make a Skimming-dish of his Skull: I know your Genius can interpret my meaning. The people of this place (whether the saltness of the Ocean gave them any alteration when they went over first, or their continual dwelling under the remote Clyme where they now inhabit, I know not) are a more acute people in general, in matters of Trade and Commerce, then in any other place of the World (see note No. 60), and by their crafty and sure bargaining, do often over-reach the raw and unexperienced Merchant. To be short, he that undertakes Merchants imployment for *Mary-Land,* must have more of Knave in him then Fool; he must not be a windling piece of Formality, that will lose his Imployers Goods for Conscience sake; nor a flashy piece of Prodigality, that will give his Merchants fine Hollands, Laces, and Silks, to purchase the benevolence of a Female : But he must be a man of solid confidence, carrying alwayes in his looks the Effigies of an Execution upon Command, if he supposes a baffle or denyal of payment, where a debt for his Imployer is legally due. (See note No. 61).

Sir, I had like almost to forgot to tell you in what part of the World I am : I dwell by providence Servant to Mr. *Thomas Stocket* (see note No. 62), in the County of *Baltemore,* within the Province of *Mary-Land,* under the Government of the Lord *Baltemore,* being a Country abounding with the variety and diversity of all that is or may be rare. But lest I should Tantalize you with a relation of that which is very unlikely of your enjoying, by reason of that strong Antipathy you have ever had 'gainst Travel, as to your own particular : I'le only tell you, that *Mary-Land* is seated within the large extending armes of *America,* between the Degrees of 36 and 38, being in Longitude from *England* eleven hundred and odd Leagues.

Vale.

G. A.

From *Mary-Land, Jan.* 17. *Anno*

To my Honored Friend Mr. T. B. *at his House.*

SIR,

YOurs I received, wherein I find my self much obliged to you for your good opinion of me, I return you millions of thanks.

Sir, you wish me well, and I pray God as well that those wishes may light upon me, and then I question not but all will do well. Those Pictures you sent sewed up in a Pastboard, with a Letter tacked on the outside, you make no mention at all what should be done with them: If they are Saints, unless I knew their names, I could make no use of them. Pray in your next let me know what they are, for my fingers itch to be doing with them one way or another. Our Government here hath had a small fit of a Rebellious Quotidian, (see note No. 63), but five Grains of the powder of Subvertment has qualified it. Pray be larger in your next how things stand in *England:* I understand His Majesty is return'd with Honour, and seated in the hereditary Throne of his Father; God

bless him from Traytors, and the Church from Sacri-
legious Schisms, and you as a loyal Subject to the
one, and a true Member to the other; while you so
continue, the God of order, peace and tranquility,
bless and preserve you, *Amen.*

Vale.

Your real Friend,

G. A.

From *Mary-Land*, Febr. 20. *Anno*

To my Honored Father at his House.

Sir,

With a twofold unmeasurable joy I received
your Letter: First, in the consideration of
Gods great Mercy to you in particular, (though weak
and aged) yet to give you dayes among the living.
Next, that his now most Excellent Majesty *Charles*
the Second, is by the omnipotent Providence of God,
seated in the Throne of his Father. I hope that God
has placed him there, will give him a heart to praise
and magnifie his name for ever, and a hand of just
Revenge, to punish the murthering and rebellious
Outrages of those Sons of shame and Apostacy, that
Usurped the Throne of his Sacred Honour. Near
about the time I received your Letter, (or a little
before) here sprang up in this Province of *Mary-Land*
a kind of pigmie Rebellion: A company of weak-

witted men, which thought to have traced the steps of *Oliver* in Rebellion (see note No. 63). They began to be mighty stiff and hidebound in their proceedings, clothing themselves with the flashy pretences of future and imaginary honour, and (had they not been suddenly quell'd) they might have done so much mischief (for aught I know) that nothing but utter ruine could have ransomed their headlong follies.

His Majesty appearing in *England*, he quickly (by the splendor of his Rayes) thawed the stiffness of their frozen and slippery intentions. All things (blessed be God for it) are at peace and unity here now: And as *Luther* being asked once, What he thought of some small Opinions that started up in his time? answered, *That he thought them to be good honest people, exempting their error:* So I judge of these men, That their thoughts were not so bad at first, as their actions would have led them into in process of time.

I have here enclosed sent you something written in haste upon the Kings coming to the enjoyment of his Throne, with a reflection upon the former sad and bad times; I have done them as well as I could, considering all things: If they are not so well as they should be, all I can do is to wish them better for your sakes. My Obedience to you and my Mother alwayes devoted.

Your Son

G. A.

From *Mary-Land*, Febr. 9. *Anno*

To my Cosen Mris. Ellinor Evins.

E' *re I forget the Zenith of your Love,*
L *et me be banisht from the Thrones above;*
L *ight let me never see, when I grow rude,*
I *ntomb your Love in base Ingratitude:*
N *or may I prosper, but the state*
O *f gaping* Tantalus *be my fate;*
R *ather then I should thus preposterous grow,*
E *arth would condemn me to her vaults below.*
V *ertuous and Noble, could my Genius raise*
I *mmortal Anthems to your Vestal praise,*
N *one should be more laborious than I,*
S *aint-like to Canonize you to the Sky.*

The Antimonial Cup (dear Cosen) you sent me, I had; and as soon as I received it, I went to work with the Infirmities and Diseases of my body. At the first draught, it made such havock among the several humors that had stolen into my body, that like a Conjurer in a room among a company of little Devils, they no sooner hear him begin to speak high words, but away they pack, and happy is he that can get out first, some up the Chimney, and the rest down stairs, till they are all disperst. So those malignant humors of my body, feeling the operative power, and medicinal virtue of this Cup, were so amazed at their sudden surprizal, (being alwayes before battered only by the weak assaults of some few Empyricks) they stood not long to dispute, but with joynt consent made their retreat, some running through the sink of the Skullery, the rest climbing up my ribs, took my mouth for a Garret-window, and so leapt out.

Cosen, For this great kindness of yours, in sending me this medicinal vertue, I return you my thanks: It came in a very good time, when I was dangerously sick, and by the assistance of God it hath perfectly recovered me.

I have sent you here a few Furrs, they were all I could get at present, I humbly beg your acceptance of them, as a pledge of my love and thankfulness unto you; I subscribe,

Your loving Cosen,

G. A.

From *Mary Land, Dec. 9. Anno*

To My Brother P. A.

BROTHER,

I Have made a shift to unloose my self from my Collar now as well as you, but I see at present either small pleasure or profit in it: What the futurality of my dayes will bring forth, I know not; For while I was linckt with the Chain of a restraining Servitude, I had all things cared for, and now I have all things to care for my self, which makes me almost to wish my self in for the other four years.

Liberty without money, is like a man opprest with the Gout, every step he puts forward puts him to pain; when on the other side, he that has Coyn with his Liberty, is like the swift Post-Messenger of the Gods, that wears wings at his heels, his motion being swift or slow, as he pleaseth.

I received this year two Caps, the one white, of an honest plain countenance, the other purple, which I conceive to be some antient Monumental Relique; which of them you sent I know not, and it was a wonder how I should, for there was no mention in the Letter, more then, *that my Brother had sent me a Cap:* They were delivered me in the company of some Gentlemen that ingaged me to write a few lines upon the purple one, and because they were my Friends I could not deny them; and here I present them to you as they were written.

Haile from the dead, or from Eternity,
Thou Velvit Relique of Antiquity;
Thou which appear'st here in thy purple hew,
Tell's how the dead within their Tombs do doe;
How those Ghosts fare within each Marble Cell,
Where amongst them for Ages thou didst dwell.
What Brain didst cover there? tell us that we
Upon our knees vayle Hats to honour thee:
And if no honour's due, tell us whose pate
Thou basely coveredst, and we'l joyntly hate:
Let's know his name, that we may shew neglect;
If otherwise, we'l kiss thee with respect.
Say, didst thou cover Noll's old brazen head,
Which on the top of Westminster high Lead

Stands on a Pole, erected to the sky,
As a grand Trophy to his memory.
From his perfidious skull didst thou fall down,
In a dis-dain to honour such a crown
With three-pile Velvet? tell me, hadst thou thy fall
From the high top of that Cathedral?
None of the Heroes of the Roman stem,
Wore ever such a fashion'd Diadem,
Didst thou speak Turkish in thy unknown dress,
Thou'dst cover Great Mogull, and no man less;
But in thy make methinks thou'rt too too scant,
To be so great a Monarch's Turberant.
The Jews by Moses swear, they never knew
E're such a Cap drest up in Hebrew:
Nor the strict Order of the Romish See,
Wears any Cap that looks so base as thee;
His Holiness hates thy Lowness, and instead,
Wears Peters spired Steeple on his head:
The Cardinals descent is much more flat,
For want of name, baptized is A Hat;
Through each strict Order has my fancy ran,
Both Ambrose, Austin, and the Franciscan,
Where I beheld rich Images of the dead,
Yet scarce had one a Cap upon his head:
Episcopacy wears Caps, but not like thee,
Though several shap'd, with much diversity:
'Twere best I think I presently should gang
To Edenburghs strict Presbyterian;
But Caps they've none, their ears being made so large,
Serves them to turn it like a Garnesey Barge;
Those keep their skulls warm against North-west gusts,
When they in Pulpit do poor Calvin curse.

Thou art not Fortunatus, *for I daily see,*
That which I wish is farthest off from me:
Thy low-built state none ever did advance,
To christen thee the Cap of Maintenance;
Then till I know from whence thou didst derive,
Thou shalt be call'd, the Cap of Fugitive.

You writ to me this year to send you some Smoak; at that instant it made me wonder that a man of a rational Soul, having both his eyes (blessed be God) should make so unreasonable a demand, when he that has but one eye, nay he which has never a one, and is fain to make use of an Animal conductive for his optick guidance, cannot endure the prejudice that Smoak brings with it: But since you are resolv'd upon it, I'le dispute it no further.

I have sent you that which will make Smoak, (namely Tobacco) though the Funk it self is so slippery that I could not send it, yet I have sent you the Substance from whence the Smoak derives: What use you imploy it to I know not, nor will I be too importunate to know; yet let me tell you this, That if you burn it in a room to affright the Devil from the house, you need not fear but it will work the same effect, as *Tobyes* galls did upon the leacherous Fiend.   No more at present.   *Vale.*

Your Brother,

G. A.

From *Mary-Land, Dec.* 11. *Anno*

To my Honored Friend Mr. T. B.

Sir,

THis is the entrance upon my fifth year, and I fear 'twill prove the worst: I have been very much troubled with a throng of unruly Distempers, that have (contrary to my expectation) crouded into the Main-guard of my body, when the drowsie Sentinels of my brain were a sleep. Where they got in I know not, but to my grief and terror I find them predominant: Yet as Doctor *Dunne*, sometimes Dean of St. *Pauls, said, That the bodies diseases do but mellow a man for Heaven, and so ferments him in this World, as he shall need no long concoction in the Grave, but hasten to the Resurrection.* And if this were weighed seriously in the Ballance of Religious Reason, the World we dwell in would not seem so inticing and bewitching as it doth.

We are only sent by God of an Errand into this World, and the time that's allotted us for to stay, is only for an Answer. When God my great Master shall in good earnest call me home, which these warnings tell me I have not long to stay, I hope then I shall be able to give him a good account of my Message.

Sir, My weakness gives a stop to my writing, my hand being so shakingly feeble, that I can hardly hold my pen any further then to tell you, I am yours

14   513

while I live, which I believe will be but some few minutes.

If this Letter come to you before I'me dead, pray for me, but if I am gone, pray howsoever, for they can do me no harm if they come after me.

Vale.

Your real Friend,

G. A.

From *Mary-Land*, Dec. 13. *Anno*

To my Parents.

FRom the Grave or Receptacle of Death am I raised, and by an omnipotent power made capable of offering once more my Obedience (that lies close cabbined in the inwardmost apartment of my Soul) at the feet of your immutable Loves.

My good Parents, God hath done marvellous things for me, far beyond my deserts, which at best were preposterously sinful, and unsuitable to the sacred will of an Almighty : *But he is merciful, and his mercy endures for ever.* When sinful man has by his Evils and Iniquities pull'd some penetrating Judgment upon his head, and finding himself immediately not able to stand under so great a burthen as Gods smallest stroke of Justice, lowers the Top-gallant sayle of his Pride, and with an humble submissiveness prostrates himself before the Throne of his sacred Mercy, and like those three Lepars that sate at the Gate of *Samaria,* resolved, *If we go into the City we shall perish, and if we stay here we shall perish also : Therefore we will throw our selves into the hands of the* Assyrians *and if we perish, we perish :* This was just my condition as to eternal state; my soul was at a stand in this black storm of affliction : I view'd the World, and all that's pleasure in her, and found her altogether flashy, aiery, and full of notional pretensions, and not one firm place where a distressed Soul could hang his trust on. Next I viewed my self, and there I found, instead of good Works, lively Faith, and Charity, a most horrid neast of condemned Evils, bearing a supreme Prerogative over my internal faculties. You'l say here was little hope of rest in this extreme Eclipse, being in a desperate amaze to see my estate so deplorable : My better Angel urged me to deliver up my aggrievances to the Bench of Gods Mercy, the sure support of all distressed Souls : His Heavenly warning, and inward whispers of the good Spirit I was resolv'd to entertain, and not quench, and throw my self into the armes of a loving God, *If I perish, I perish.* 'Tis beyond wonder to think of the love of God extended to sinful man, that in the deepest distresses or agonies of Affliction, when all other things prove rather hinderances then advantages, even at that time God is ready and steps forth to the supportment of his drooping Spirit. Truly, about a fortnight before I wrote this Letter, two of our ablest Physicians rendered me up into the hands of God, the universal Doctor of the whole World, and subscribed with a silent acknowledgement, That all their Arts, screw'd up to the very Zenith of Scholastique perfection, were not capable of keeping me from the Grave at that time : But God, the great preserver of Soul and Body, said contrary to the expectation of humane reason, *Arise, take up thy bed and walk.*

I am now (through the help of my Maker) creeping up to my former strength and vigour, and every day I live, I hope I shall, through the assistance of divine Grace, climbe nearer and nearer to my eternal home.

I have received this year three Letters from you, one by Capt. *Conway* Commander of the *Wheat-Sheaf,* the others by a *Bristol* Ship.   Having no more at present to trouble you with, but expecting your promise, I remain as ever,

Your dutiful Son,

G. A.

Mary-Land, April 9. *Anno*

I desire my hearty love may be remembered to my Brother, and the rest of my Kinred.

FINIS.

NOTES.

Note 1, page 15.

After having resolved to reprint Alsop's early account of Maryland, as an addition to my *Bibliotheca Americana*, I immediately fell in with a difficulty which I had not counted on. After much inquiry and investigation, I could find no copy to print from among all my earnest book collecting acquaintances. At length some one informed me that Mr. Bancroft the historian had a copy in his library. I immediately took the liberty of calling on him and making known my wants, he generously offered to let me have the use of it for the purpose stated, I carried the book home, had it carefully copied, but unfortunately during the process I discovered the text was imperfect as well as deficient in both portrait and map. Like Sisyphus I had to begin anew, and do nearly all my labor over; I sent to London to learn if the functionaries in the British Museum would permit a tracing of the portrait and map to be made from their copy, the answer returned was, that they would or could not permit this, but I might perfect my text if I so choosed by copying from theirs. Here I was once more at sea without compass, rudder, or chart: I made known my condition to an eminent and judicious collector of old American literature in the city of New York, he very frankly informed me that he could aid me in my difficulty by letting me have the use of a copy, which would relieve me from my present dilemma. I was greatly rejoiced at this discovery as well as by the generosity of the owner. The following day the book was put into my possession, and so by the aid of it was enabled to complete the text. Here another difficulty burst into view, this copy had no portrait. That being the only defect in perfecting a copy of Alsop's book, I now resolved to proceed and publish it without a portrait, but perhaps fortunately, making known this resolve to some of the knowing ones in book gathering, they remonstrated against this course, adding that it would ruin the book in the estimation of all who would buy such a rarity. I was inclined to listen favorably to this protest, and therefore had to commence a new effort to obtain a portrait. I then laid about me again to try and procure a copy that had one: I knew that not more than three or four collectors in the country who were likely to have such an heir-loom. To one living at a considerable distance from New York I took the liberty of addressing a letter on the subject, wherein I made known my difficulties. To my great gratification this courteous and confiding gentleman not only immediately made answer, but sent a perfect copy of this rare and much wanted book for my use. I immediately had the portrait and map reproduced by the photo-lithographic process. During the time the book was in my possession, which was about ten days, so fearful was I that any harm should befall it that I took the precaution to wrap up the precious little volume in tissue paper and carry it about with me all the time in my side pocket, well knowing that if it was either injured or lost I could not replace it. I understand that a perfect copy of the original in the London market would bring fifty pounds sterling. I had the satisfaction to learn it reached the generous owner in safety.

Had I known the difficulties I had to encounter of procuring a copy of the original of Alsop's singular performance, I most certainly would never have undertaken to reproduce it in America. Mr. Jared Sparks told me that he had a like difficulty to encounter when he undertook to write the life of Ledyard the traveler. Said he: "a copy of his journal I could find nowhere to purchase, at length I was compelled to borrow a copy on very humiliating conditions; the owner perhaps valued it too highly." I may add that I had nearly as much difficulty in securing an editor, as I had in procuring a perfect copy. However on this point I at last was very fortunate.

WILLIAM GOWANS.

115 Nassau street, March 23d, 1869.

Note 2, page 19.

Cecilius, Lord Baltimore, eldest son of George Calvert, 1st Lord Baltimore, and Anne Wynne of Hertingfordbury, England, was born in 1606. He succeeded to the title April 15, 1632, and married Anne, daughter of Lord Arundel, whose name was given to a county in Maryland. His rule over Maryland, disturbed in Cromwell's time, but restored under Charles II, has always been extolled. He died Nov. 30, 1675, covered with age and reputation.—*O'Callaghan's N. Y. Col. Doc.*, II. p. 74.

Note 3, page 19.

Avalon, the territory in Newfoundland, of which the first Lord Baltimore obtained a grant in 1623, derived its name from the spot in England where, as tradition said, Christianity was first preached by Joseph of Arimathea.

Note 4, page 21.

Owen Feltham, as our author in his errata correctly gives the name, was an author who enjoyed a great reputation in his day. His *Resolves* appeared first about 1620, and in 1696 had reached the eleventh edition. They were once reprinted in the 18th century, and in full or in part four times in the

19th, and an edition appeared in America about 1830. Hallam in spite of this popularity calls him "labored, artificial and shallow."

Note 5, page 24.

Burning on the hand was not so much a punishment as a mark on those who, convicted of felony, pleaded the benefit of clergy, which they were allowed to do once only.

Note 6, page 25.

Literally: "Good wine needs no sign."

Note 7, page 26.

Billingsgate is the great fish market of London, and the scurrilous tongues of the fish women have made the word synonymous with vulgar abuse.

Note 8, page 28.

Alsop though cautiously avoiding Maryland politics, omits no fling at the Puritans. Pride was a parliament colonel famous for *Pride's Purge.*

Notes 9, 10, pages 31, 33.

William Bogherst, and H. W., Master of Arts, have eluded all our efforts to immortalize them.

Note 11, page 35.

Chesapeake is said to be K'tchisipik, Great Water, in Algonquin.

Note 12, page 38.

Less bombast and some details as to the botany of Maryland would have been preferable.

Note 13, page 39.

The American deer (*Cariacus Virginianus*) is here evidently meant.

Note 14, page 39.

Whetston's (Whetstone) park : " A dilapidated street in Lincoln's Inn Fields, at the back of Holborn.   It contains scarcely anything but old, half-tumble down houses ; not a living plant of any kind adorns its nakedness, so it is presumable that as a park it never had an existence, or one so remote that even tradition has lost sight of the fact."

Note 15, page 39.

The animals here mentioned are the black wolf (*canis occidentalis*), the black bear, the panther (*felis concolor*).

Note 16, page 40.

These animals are well known, the elk (*alces Americanus*), cat o' the mountain or catamount (*felis concolor*), raccoon (*procyon lotor*), fox (*vulpes fulvus*), beaver (*castor fiber*), otter (*lutra*), opossum (*didelphys Virginiana*), hare, squirrel, musk-rat (*fiber zibethicus*).   The monack is apparently the Maryland marmot or woodchuck (*arctomys monax*).

Note 17, page 40.

The domestic animals came chiefly from Virginia.   As early as May 27, 1634, they got 100 swine from Accomac, with 30 cows, and they expected goats and hens (*Relation of Maryland*, 1634).   Horses and sheep had to be imported from England, Virginia being unable to give any.   Yet in 1679 Dankers and Sluyters, the Labadists, say : " Sheep they have none."— *Collections Long Island Hist. Soc.*, I, p. 218.

Note 18, page 41.

Alluding to the herds of swine kept by the Gadarenes, into one of which the Saviour allowed the devil named Legion to enter.

Note 19, page 42.

The abundance of these birds is mentioned in the *Relations of Maryland*, 1634, p. 22, and 1635, p. 23.   The Labadists with whose travels the Hon.

H. C. Murphy has enriched our literature, found the geese in 1679–80 so plentiful and noisy as to prevent their sleeping, and the ducks filling the sky like a cloud.—*Long Island Hist. Coll.*, I, pp. 195, 204.

Note 20, page 43.

Alsop makes no allusion to the cultivation of maize, yet the Labadists less than twenty years after describe it at length as the principal grain crop of Maryland.—*Ib.*, p. 216.

Note 21, page 45.

Considering the facts of history, this picture is sadly overdrawn, Maryland having had its full share of civil war.

Note 22, page 46.

The fifth monarchy men were a set of religionists who arose during the Puritan rule in England. They believed in a fifth universal monarchy of which Christ was to be the head, under whom they, his saints, were to possess the earth. In 1660 they caused an outbreak in London, in which many were killed and others tried and executed. Their leader was one Venner. The Adamites, a gnostic sect, who pretended that regenerated man should go naked like Adam and Eve in their state of innocence, were revived during the Puritan rule in England; and in our time in December, 1867, we have seen the same theory held and practiced in Newark, N. J.

Note 23, page 46.

In the provisional act, passed in the first assembly, March 19, 1638, and entitled "An Act ordaining certain laws for the government of this province," the twelfth section required that "every person planting tobacco shall plant and tend two acres of corn." A special act was introduced the same session and read twice, but not passed. A new law was passed, however, Oct. 23, 1640, renewed Aug. 1, 1642, April 21, 1649, Oct. 20, 1654, April 12, 1662, and made perpetual in 1676. These acts imposed a fine of fifty pounds of tobacco for every half acre the offender fell short, besides fifty pounds of the same current leaf as constables' fees. It was to this persistent enforcement of the cultivation of cereals that Maryland so soon became the granary of New England.

Note 24, *page* 47.

The Assembly, or House of Burgesses, at first consisted of all freemen, but they gradually gave place to delegates. The influence of the proprietary, however, decided the selection. In 1650 fourteen burgesses met as delegates or representatives of the several hundreds, there being but two counties organized, St. Marys and the Isle of Kent. Ann Arundel, called at times Providence county, was erected April 29, 1650. Patuxent was erected under Cromwell in 1654.—*Bacon's Laws of Maryland*, 1765.

Note 25, *page* 47.

Things had changed when the *Sot Weed Factor* appeared, as the author of that satirical poem dilates on the litigious character of the people.

Note 26, *page* 47.

The allusion here I have been unable to discover.

Note 27, *page* 48.

The colony seems to have justified some of this eulogy by its good order, which is the more remarkable, considering the height of party feeling.

Note 28, *page* 48.

Halberdeers; the halberd was smaller than the partisan, with a sharp pointed blade, with a point on one side like a pole-axe.

Note 29, *page* 49.

Newgate, Ludgate and Bridewell are the well known London prisons.

Note 30, *page* 50.

Our author evidently failed from this cause.

Note 31, page 50.

A fling at the various Puritan schools, then active at home and abroad.

Note 32, page 50.

The first Quakers in Maryland were Elizabeth Harris, Josiah Cole, and Thomas Thurston, who visited it in 1657, but as early as July 23, 1659, the governor and council issued an order to seize any Quakers and whip them from constable to constable out of the province. Yet in spite of this they had settled meetings as early as 1661, and Peter Sharpe, the Quaker physician, appears as a landholder in 1665, the very year of Alsop's publication.—*Norris, Early Friends or Quakers in Maryland* (Maryland Hist. Soc., March, 1862).

Note 33, page 50.

The Baptists centering in Rhode Island, extended across Long Island to New Jersey, and thence to New York city ; but at this time had not reached the south.

Note 34, page 56.

A copy of the usual articles is given in the introduction. Alsop here refutes current charges against the Marylanders for their treatment of servants. Hammond, in his *Leah and Rachel*, p. 12, says : " The labour servants are put to is not so hard, nor of such continuance as husbandmen nor handecraftmen are kept at in England. . . . . The women are not (as is reported) put into the ground to worke, but occupie such domestic imployments and housewifery as in England."

Note 35, page 59.

Laws as to the treatment of servants were passed in the Provisional act of 1638, and at many subsequent assemblies.

Notes 36, 37, pages 59, 61.

Lewknors lane or Charles street was in Drury lane, in the parish of St. Giles.—*Seymour's History of London*, II, p. 767. Finsbury is still a well known quarter, in St. Luke's parish, Middlesex.

Note 38, page 65.

Nicholas Culpepper, "student in physic and astrology," whose *English Physician*, published in 1652, ran through many editions, and is still a book published and sold.

Note 39, page 65.

Dogs dung, used in dressing morocco, is euphemized into *album græcum*, and is also called *pure ;* those who gather it being still styled in England pure-finders.—*Mayhew, London Labor and London Poor*, ii, p. 158.

Note 40, page 65.

He has not mentioned tobacco as a crop, but describes it fully a few pages after. In Maryland as in Virginia it was the currency. Thus in 1638 an act authorized the erection of a water-mill to supersede hand-mills for grinding grain, and the cost was limited to 20,000 lbs. of tobacco.—*McSherry's History of Maryland*, p. 56. The Labadists in their *Travels* (p. 216) describe the cultivation at length. Tobacco at this time paid two shillings English a cask export duty in Maryland, and two-pence a pound duty on its arrival in England, besides weighing and other fees.

Note 41, page 66.

The Parson of Pancras is unknown to me : but the class he represents is certainly large.

Note 42, page 66.

The buffalo was not mentioned in the former list, and cannot be considered as synonymous with elk.

Note 43, page 67.

For satisfactory and correct information of the present commerce and condition of Maryland, the reader is referred to the *Census of the United States* in 4 vols., 4to, published at Washington, 1865.

Note 44, *page* 69.

This is a curious observation as to New England trade. A century later Hutchinson represents Massachusetts as receiving Maryland flour from the Pennsylvania mills, and paying in money and bills of exchange.—*Hist. of Massachusetts*, p. II, 397.

Note 45, *page* 69.

The trade with Barbadoes, now insignificant, was in our colonial times of great importance to all the colonies. Barbadoes is densely peopled and thoroughly cultivated ; its imports and exports are each about five millions of dollars annually.

Note 46, *page* 71.

The Susquehannas. This *Relation* is one of the most valuable portions of Alsop's tract, as no other Maryland document gives as much concerning this tribe, which nevertheless figures extensively in Maryland annals. Dutch and Swedish writers speak of a tribe called Minquas (Minquosy, Machœretini in *De Laet*, p. 76); the French in Canada (*Champlain*, the *Jesuit Relations, Gendron, Particularitez du Pays des Hurons*, p. 7, etc.), make frequent allusion to the Gandastogués (more briefly Andastés), a tribe friendly to their allies the Hurons, and sturdy enemies of the Iroquois ; later still Pennsylvania writers speak of the Conestogas, the tribe to which Logan belonged, and the tribe which perished at the hands of the Paxton boys. Although Gallatin in his map, followed by Bancroft, placed the Andastés near Lake Erie, my researches led me to correct this, and identify the Susquehannas, Minqua, Andastés or Gandastogués and Conestogas as being all the same tribe, the first name being apparently an appellation given them by the Virginia tribes ; the second that given them by the Algonquins on the Delaware ; while Gandastogué as the French, or Conestoga as the English wrote it, was their own tribal name, meaning cabin-pole men, *Natio Perticarum*, from Andasta, a cabin-pole (map in Creuxius, *Historia Canadensis*). I forwarded a paper on the subject to Mr. Schoolcraft, for insertion in the government work issuing under his supervision. It was inserted in the last volume without my name, and ostensibly as Mr. Schoolcraft's. I then gave it with my name in the *Historical Magazine*, vol. II, p. 294. The result arrived at there has been accepted by Bancroft, in his large paper edition, by Parkman, in his *Jesuits in the Wilderness*, by Dr. O'Callaghan, S. F. Streeter, Esq., of the Maryland Historical Society, and students generally.

From the Virginian, Dutch, Swedish and French authorities, we can thus give their history briefly.

The territory now called Canada, and most of the northern portion of the United States, from Lake Superior and the Mississippi to the mouth of the St. Lawrence and Chesapeake bay were, when discovered by Europeans, occupied by two families of tribes, the Algonquin and the Huron Iroquois. The former which included all the New England tribes, the Micmacs, Mohegans, Delawares, Illinois, Chippewas, Ottawas, Pottawatamies, Sacs, Foxes, Miamis, and many of the Maryland and Virginian tribes surrounded the more powerful and civilized tribes who have been called Huron Iroquois, from the names of the two most powerful nations of the group, the Hurons or Wyandots of Upper Canada, and the Iroquois or Five Nations of New York. Besides these the group included the Neuters on the Niagara, the Dinondadies in Upper Canada, the Eries south of the lake of that name, the Andastogués or Susquehannas on that river, the Nottaways and some other Virginian tribes, and finally the Tuscaroras in North Carolina and perhaps the Cherokees, whose language presents many striking points of similarity.

Both these groups of tribes claimed a western origin, and seem, in their progress east, to have driven out of Ohio the Quappas, called by the Algonquins, Alkansas or Allegewi, who retreated down the Ohio and Mississippi to the district which has preserved the name given them by the Algonquins.

After planting themselves on the Atlantic border, the various tribes seem to have soon divided and become embroiled in war. The Iroquois, at first inferior to the Algonquins were driven out of the valley of the St. Lawrence into the lake region of New York, where by greater cultivation, valor and union they soon became superior to the Algonquins of Canada and New York, as the Susquehannas who settled on the Susquehanna did over the tribes in New Jersey, Maryland and Virginia. (*Du Ponceau's Campanius*, p. 158.) Prior to 1600 the Susquehannas and the Mohawks, the most eastern Iroquois tribe, came into collision, and the Susquehannas nearly exterminated the Mohawks in a war which lasted ten years. (*Relation de la Nouv. France*, 1659–60, p. 28.)

In 1608 Captain Smith, in exploring the Chesapeake and its tributaries, met a party of sixty of these Sasquesahanocks as he calls them (I, p. 120–1), and he states that they were still at war with the Massawomekes or Mohawks. (*De Laet Novus Orbis*, p. 79.)

DeVries, in his *Voyages* (Murphy's translation, p. 41–3), found them in 1633 at war with the Armewamen and Sankiekans, Algonquin tribes on the Delaware, maintaining their supremacy by butchery. They were friendly to the Dutch. When the Swedes in 1638 settled on the Delaware, they renewed the friendly intercourse begun by the Dutch. They purchased lands of the ruling tribe and thus secured their friendship. (*Hazard's Annals*, p. 48). They carried the terror of their arms southward also, and in 1634 to 1644 they waged war on the Yaomacoes, the Piscataways and Patuxents (*Bozman's Maryland*, II, p. 161), and were so troublesome that in 1642 Governor Calvert, by proclamation, declared them public enemies.

When the Hurons in Upper Canada in 1647 began to sink under the fearful blows dealt by the Five Nations, the Susquehannas sent an embassy to offer them aid against the common enemy. (*Gendron, Quelques Particularitez du Pays des Hurons*, p. 7), Nor was the offer one of little value, for the Susquehannas could put in the field 1,300 warriors (*Relation de la Nouvelle France*, 1647–8, p. 58) trained to the use of fire arms and European modes of war by three Swedish soldiers whom they had obtained to instruct them. (*Proud's Pennsylvania*, I, p. 111; *Bozman's Maryland*, II, p. 273. Before interposing in the war, they began by negotiation, and sent an embassy to Onondaga to urge the cantons to peace. (*Relation*, 1648, p. 58). The Iroquois refused, and the Hurons, sunk in apathy, took no active steps to secure the aid of the friendly Susquehannas.

That tribe, however, maintained its friendly intercourse with its European neighbors, and in 1652 Sawahegeh, Auroghteregh, Scarhuhadigh, Rutchogah and Nathheldianeh, in presence of a Swedish deputy, ceded to Maryland all the territory from the Patuxent river to Palmer's island, and from the Choptauk to the northeast branch north of Elk river. (*Bozman's Maryland*, II, p. 683).

Four years later the Iroquois, grown insolent by their success in almost annihilating their kindred tribes north and south of Lake Erie, the Wyandots, Dinondadies, Neuters and Eries, provoked a war with the Susquehannas, plundering their hunters on Lake Ontario. (*Relation de la Nouvelle France*, 1657, pp. 11, 18).

It was at this important period in their history that Alsop knew and described them to us.

In 1661 the small-pox, that scourge of the native tribes, broke out in their town, sweeping off many and enfeebling the nation terribly. War had now begun in earnest with the Five Nations; and though the Susquehannas had some of their people killed near their town (*Hazard's Annals*, 341–7), they in turn pressed the Cayugas so hard that some of them retreated across Lake Ontario to Canada (*Relation de la Nouvelle France*, 1661, p. 39, 1668, p. 20). They also kept the Senecas in such alarm that they no longer ventured to carry their peltries to New York, except in caravans escorted by six hundred men, who even took a most circuitous route. (*Relation*, 1661, p. 40). A law of Maryland passed May 1, 1661, authorized the governor to aid the Susquehannas.

Smarting under constant defeat, the Five Nations solicited French aid (*Relation de la Nouvelle France*, 1662–3, p. 11, 1663–4, p. 33 ; *Charlevoix*, II, p. 134), but in April, 1663, the Western cantons raised an army of eight hundred men to invest and storm the fort of the Susquehannas. They embarked on Lake Ontario, according to the French account, and then went overland to the Susquehanna. On reaching the fort, however, they found

it well defended on the river side, and on the land side with two bastions in
European style with cannon mounted and connected by a double curtain of
large trees. After some trifling skirmishes the Iroquois had recourse to
stratagem. They sent in a party of twenty-five men to treat of peace and
ask provisions to enable them to return. The Susquehannas admitted them,
but immediately burned them all alive before the eyes of their countrymen.
(*Relation de la Nouvelle France*, 1663, p. 10). The Pennsylvania writers,
(*Hazard's Annals of Pennsylvania*, p. 346) make the Iroquois force one
thousand six hundred, and that of the Susquehannas only one hundred.
They add that when the Iroquois retreated, the Susquehannas pursued
them, killing ten and taking as many.

After this the war was carried on in small parties, and Susquehanna
prisoners were from time to time burned at Oneida, Onondaga, Seneca and
Cayuga (*Relations de la Nouvelle France*, 1668 to 1673), and their prisoners
doubtless at Canoge on the Susquehanna. In the fall of 1669 the Susquehannas, after defeating the Cayugas, offered peace, but the Cayugas put
their ambassador and his nephew to death, after retaining him five or six
months; the Oneidas having taken nine Susquehannas and sent some to
Cayuga, with forty wampum belts to maintain the war. (*Relation de la
Nouvelle France*, 1670, p. 68.)

At this time the great war chief of the Susquehannas was one styled
Hochitagete or Barefoot (*Relation de la Nouvelle France*, 1670, p. 47); and
raving women and crafty medicine men deluded the Iroquois with promises
of his capture and execution at the stake (*Relation*, 1670, p. 47), and a
famous medicine man of Oneida appeared after death to order his body to
be taken up and interred on the trail leading to the Susquehannas as the
only means of saving that canton from ruin. (*Relation*, 1672, p. 20.)

Towards the summer of 1672 a body of forty Cayugas descended the
Susquehanna in canoes, and twenty Senecas went by land to attack the
Susquehannas in their fields; but a band of sixty Andasté or Susquehanna
boys, the oldest not over sixteen, attacked the Senecas, and routed them,
killing one brave and taking another. Flushed with victory they pushed
on to attack the Cayugas, and defeated them also, killing eight and wound-
ing with arrow, knife and hatchet, fifteen or sixteen more, losing, however,
fifteen or sixteen of their gallant band. (*Relation*, 1672, p. 24.)

At this time the Susquehannas or Andastés were so reduced by war and
pestilence that they could muster only three hundred warriors. In 1675,
however, the Susquehannas were completely overthrown (*Etat Present*,
1675, manuscript; *Relation*, 1676, p. 2; *Relations Inédites*, II, p. 44; *Col-
den's Five Nations*, I, p. 126), but unfortunately we have no details whatever
as to the forces which effected it, or the time or manner of their utter defeat.

A party of about one hundred retreated into Maryland, and occupied
some abandoned Indian forts. Accused of the murder of some settlers,
apparently slain by the Senecas, they sent five of their chiefs to the Mary-
land and Virginia troops, under Washington and Brent, who went out in

pursuit. Although coming as deputies, and showing the Baltimore medal and certificate of friendship, these chiefs were cruelly put to death. The enraged Susquehannas then began a terrible border war, which was kept till their utter destruction (S. F. Streeter's Destruction of the Susquehannas, *Historical Magazine*, I, p. 65). The rest of the tribe, after making overtures to Lord Baltimore, submitted to the Five Nations, and were allowed to retain their ancient grounds. When Pennsylvania was settled, they became known as Conestogas, and were always friendly to the colonists of Penn, as they had been to the Dutch and Swedes. In 1701 Canoodagtoh, their king, made a treaty with Penn, and in the document they are styled Minquas, Conestogos or Susquehannas. They appear as a tribe in a treaty in 1742, but were dwindling away. In 1763 the feeble remnant of the tribe became involved in the general suspicion entertained by the colonists against the red men, arising out of massacres on the borders. To escape danger the poor creatures took refuge in Lancaster jail, and here they were all butchered by the Paxton boys, who burst into the place. Parkman in his *Conspiracy of Pontiac*, p. 414, details the sad story.

The last interest of this unfortunate tribe centres in Logan, the friend of the white man, whose speech is so familiar to all, that we must regret that it has not sustained the historical scrutiny of Brantz Mayer (*Tahgahjute; or, Logan and Capt. Michael Cresap*, Maryland Hist. Soc., May, 1851 ; and 8vo, Albany, 1867). Logan was a Conestoga, in other words a Susquehanna.

Note 47, page 71.

The language of the Susquehannas, as Smith remarks, differed from that of the Virginian tribes generally. As already stated, it was one of the dialects of the Huron-Iroquois, and its relation to other members of the family may be seen by the following table of the numerals :

	Susquehanna or Minqua.	Hochelaga.	Huron.	Mohawk.	Onondaga.
1.	Onskat,	Segada,	Eskate,	Easka,	Unskat.
2.	Tiggene,	Tigneny,	Téni,	Tekeni,	Tegni.
3.	Axe,	Asche,	Hachin,	Aghsea,	Achen.
4.	Raiene,	Honnacon,	Dac,	Kieri,	Gayeri.
5.	Wisck,	Ouiscon,	Ouyche,	Wisk,	Wisk.
6.	Jaiack,	Indahir,	Houhahea,	Yayak,	Haiak.
7.	Tzadack,	Ayaga,	Sotaret,	Jatak,	Tchiatak.
8.	Tickerom,	Addegue,	Attaret,	Satego,	Tegeron.
9.	Waderom,	Madellon,	Nechon,	Tiyohto,	Waderom,
10.	Assan,	Assem,		Oyeri.	

15

Note 48, page 73.

Smith thus describes them : " Sixty of those Sasquesahanocks came to vs with skins, Bowes, Arrows, Targets, Beads, swords and Tobacco pipes for presents.   Such great and well proportioned men are seldome seene, for they seemed like Giants to the English ; yea and to the neighbours, yet seemed of an honest and simple disposition, with much adoe restrained from adoring vs as Gods.   Those are the strangest people of all those Countries, both in language and attire ; for their language it may well beseeme their proportions, sounding from them as a voyce in a vault. Their attire is the skinnes of Beares, and Wooluues, some have Cassacks made of Beares heads and skinnes, that a mans head goes through the skinnes neck, and the eares of the Beare fastened to his shoulders, the nose and teeth hanging downe his breast, another Beares face split behind him, and at the end of the Nose hung a Pawe, the halfe sleeues comming to the elbowes were the neckes of Beares and the armes through the mouth with the pawes hanging at their noses.   One had the head of a Wolfe hanging in a chaine for a Iewell, his tobacco pipe three-quarters of a yard long, prettily carued with a Bird, a Deere or some such deuise at the great end, sufficient to beat out ones braines ; with Bowes, Arrowes and Clubs, suitable to their greatnesse.   They are scarce known to Powhatan.   They can make near 600 able men, and are palisadoed in their Townes to defend them from the Massawomekes, their mortal enemies.   Five of their chief Werowances came aboord vs and crossed the Bay in their Barge.   The picture of the greatest of them is signified in the Mappe.   The calfe of whose leg was three-quarters of a yard about, and all the rest of his limbes so answerable to that proportion, that he seemed the goodliest man we ever beheld.   His hayre, the one side was long, the other shore close with a ridge over his crowne like a cocks combe.   His arrowes were five-quarters long, headed with the splinters of a white christall-like stone, in form of a heart, an inch broad, and an inch and a halfe or more long.   These he wore in a Wooluues skinne at his backe for his quiver, his bow in one hand and his club in the other, as described."—*Smith's Voyages* (Am. ed.), I, p. 119-20. Tattooing referred to by our author, was an ancient Egyptian custom, and is still retained by the women.   See *Lane's Modern Egyptians*, etc.   It was forbidden to the Jews in *Leviticus*, 19 : 28.

Note 49, page 74.

Purchas, his Pilgrimage, or Relations of the World, and the Religions observed in all Ages and Places discovered, from the Creation unto this present," 1 vol., folio, 1613.   In spite of Alsop, Purchas is still highly esteemed.

Note 50, page 75.

As to their treatment of prisoners, see *Lafitau, Moeurs des Sauvages*, II, p. 260.

Note 51, page 75.

Smith thus locates their town : " The Sasquesahannocks inhabit vpon the cheefe spring of these foure branches of the Bayes head, one day's journey higher than our barge could passe for rocks," vol. I, p. 182. Campanius thus describes their town, which he represents as twelve miles from New Sweden : " They live on a high mountain, very steep and difficult to climb ; there they have a fort or square building, surrounded with palisades. There they have guns and small iron cannon, with which they shoot and defend themselves, and take with them when they go to war."—*Campanius's Nye Sverige*, p. 181 ; Du Ponceau's translation, p. 158. A view of a Sasquesa-hannock town is given in *Montanus, De Nieuwe en Onbekende Weereld* (1671), p. 136, based evidently on Smith. De Lisle's Map, dated June, 1718, lays down Canoge, Fort des Indiens Andastés ou Susquehanocs at about 40° N. ; but I find the name nowhere else.

Note 52, page 77.

Scalping was practiced by the Scythians. (*Herodotus*, book IV, and in the second book of *Macchabees*, VII, 4, 7). Antiochus is said to have caused two of the seven Macchabee brothers to be scalped. " The skin of the head with the hairs being drawn off." The torture of prisoners as here described originated with the Iroquois, and spread to nearly all the North American tribes. It was this that led the Algonquins to give the Iroquois tribes the names Magoué, Nadoué or Nottaway, which signified cruel. *Lafitau, Moeurs des Sauvages*, II, p. 287.

Note 53, page 78.

The remarks here as to religion are vague. The Iroquois and Hurons recognized Aireskoi or Agreskoe, as the great deity, styling him also Teharonhiawagon. As to the Hurons, see *Sagard, Histoire du Canada*, p. 485. The sacrifice of a child, as noted by Alsop, was unknown in the other tribes of this race, and is not mentioned by Campanius in regard to this one.

Note 54, page 78.

The priests were the medicine men in all probability; no author mentioning any class that can be regarded properly as priests.

Note 55, page 78.

The burial rites here described resemble those of the Iroquois (*Lafitau, Moeurs des Sauvages*, ii, pp. 389, 407) and of the Hurons, as described by Sagard (*Histoire du Canada*, p. 702) in the manner of placing the dead body in a sitting posture; but there it was wrapped in furs, encased in bark and set upon a scaffold till the feast of the dead.

Note 56, page 79.

Sagard, in his *Huron Dictionary*, gives village, *andata*; he is in the fort or village, *andatagon;* which is equivalent to *Connadago, nd* and *nn* being frequently used for each other.

Note 57, page 80.

For the condition of the women in a kindred tribe, compare *Sagard, Histoire du Canada,* p. 272; *Grand Voyage,* p. 130; *Perrot, Moeurs et Coustumes des Sauvages,* p. 30.

Note 58, page 80.

Among the Iroquois the husband elect went to the wife's cabin and sat down on the mat opposite the fire. If she accepted him she presented him a bowl of hominy and sat down beside him, turning modestly away. He then ate some and soon after retired.—*Lafitau, Moeurs des Sauvages,* i, p, 566.

Note 59, page 81.

Sagard, in his *Histoire du Canada,* p. 185, makes a similar remark as to the Hurons, a kindred tribe, men and women acting as here stated, and he says that in this they resembled the ancient Egyptians. Compare *Hennepin, Moeurs des Sauvages,* p. 54; *Description d'un Pays plus grand que l'Europe, Voyages au Nord,* v, p. 341.

Note 60, page 96.

This characteristic of the active trading propensities of the early settlers will apply to the present race of Americans in a fourfold degree.

Note 61, page 96.

One who brought goods to Maryland without following such advice as Alsop gives, describes in Hudibrastic verse his doleful story in the *Sot Weed Factor*, recently reprinted.

Note 62, page 96.

For an account of this gentleman, see ante, p. 13.

Note 63, page 97.

The rebellion in Maryland, twice alluded to by our author in his letters, was a very trifling matter. On the restoration of Charles II, Lord Baltimore sent over his brother Philip Calvert as governor, with authority to proceed against Governor Fendall, who, false alike to all parties, was now scheming to overthrow the proprietary government. The new governor was instructed on no account to permit Fendall to escape with his life ; but Philip Calvert was more clement than Lord Baltimore, and though Fendall made a fruitless effort to excite the people to opposition, he was, on his voluntary submission, punished by a merely short imprisonment. This clemency he repaid by a subsequent attempt to excite a rebellion.—*McMahon's History of Maryland*, pp. 213–14, citing Council Proceedings from 1656 to 1668, liber H. H., 74 to 82.

THE END.